THREE SIMPLE SOLUTIONS

FOR

WORLD PEACE

Grace Religious Books Publishing & Distributors, Inc.

By Grace Dola Balogun

THREE SOLUTIONS FOR WORLD PEACE
by Grace Dola Balogun

Copyright © 2012 Grace Dola Balogun
Contact Author at: www.Gracereligiousbookspublishers.com
Phone contact number: 1-646-559-2533
Grace Religious Books Publishing & Distributors, Inc.
Books may be ordered through booksellers or by contacting the publisher:

Grace Religious Books Publishing & Distributors, Inc.
213 Bennett Avenue
New York, NY 10040

All rights reserved. No part of this book may be used or reproduced by any means, graphic, electronic, or mechanical, including photocopying, recording, taping or by any information storage retrieval system without the written permission of the publisher except in the case of brief quotations embodied in critical articles and reviews.

Because of the dynamic nature of the Internet, any web addresses or links contained in this book may have changed since publication and may no longer be valid. The views expressed in this work are solely those of the author and do not necessarily reflect the views of the publisher, and the publisher hereby disclaims any responsibility for them. The author of this book does not dispense medical advice or prescribe the use of any technique as for treatment for physical, emotional, or medical problems without the advice of a physician, either directly or indirectly. The intent of the author is only to offer information of a general nature to help you in your quest for emotional and spiritual well-being. In the event you use any of the information in this book for yourself, which is your constitutional right, the author and the publisher assume no responsibility for your actions.

All Scriptures are taken from The Holy Bible, New International Version (1993).

Soft Cover ISBN 9780985971304
Hardcover ISBN: 978-0-9859713-1-1
Editing by CBM Christian Book Marketing
Cover Design by Lisa Hainline
Interior Design by CBM Christian Book Marketing
Printed in the United States of America
Grace Religious Books Publishing & Distributors, Inc.

DEDICATION

I dedicate this book to our Lord and Savior Jesus Christ, who only, is the Prince of Peace. Who has all the nations of Earth upon His shoulders. Who is the only One coming back to bring peace to this world.

I also dedicate this book to all the people on Earth who are going through long suffering and shortages of food, water and energy. I especially dedicate this book to those who are going through tribal war, nation against nation wars and civil war. May this book give comfort to those who are going through various disasters such as earthquakes, hurricanes and volcano eruptions.

I dedicate this book also to those who are going through various flood disasters such as the Myanmar Cyclone Nargis Disaster and the Japan Tsunami. I pray that they will all be comforted when the Prince of Peace returns to this Earth to judge all the nations.

Three Solutions for World Peace

TABLE OF CONTENTS

Dedication 3

Preface 9

Chapter One 11
Analysis of World Peace

Chapter Two 15
Baha'i Religion Prayer for World Peace

Chapter Three 19
Shinto Religion Prayer for World Peace

Chapter Four 23
Sikh Religion Prayer for World Peace

Chapter Five 27
Hinduism Religion Prayer for World Peace

Chapter Six 31
Buddhism Religion Prayer for World Peace

Chapter Seven 37
Zoroastrian Religion Prayer for World Peace

Chapter Eight 41
Jainism Religion Prayer for World Peace

Chapter Nine 47
Native American Religion Prayer for World Peace

Chapter Ten 57
Native African Religion Prayer for World Peace

Chapter Eleven 59
Jewish Religion Prayer for World Peace

Chapter Twelve 67
Islam Religion Prayer for World Peace

Chapter Thirteen 83
History of Ishmael and Isaac

Chapter Fourteen 89
The Roman Empire Period from 63 B.C.

Chapter Fifteen 93
The Christian Prayer for World Peace

Chapter Sixteen 97
World War II and It's Violence

Chapter Seventeen 105
United Nations Establishment and Operations

Chapter Eighteen 109
Suggestion & Advice to the Super
Power Nation Leaders & United Nations

Chapter Nineteen 119
Food Program Organization FAO & WFP Reports

Chapter Twenty 139
Statistics Facts Figures Since 2009

Chapter Twenty-One 153
Conclusion

Chapter Twenty-Two 185
Prayer For World Peace

Bibliography 188

Biblical Index 197

Qur'an Index 198

About the Author 206

Three Solutions for World Peace

PREFACE

This book is for all the people and all the inhabitants of the world, beginning with all the people who believe and practice religion, people of all religious rights, especially those who seek peace for this world. If all the people of all religious rights practice what they preach every day on the television, on the Radio, in the magazines and newspapers, the world would have been in peace more than what it is today. If people of non-religious rights live together in love there would be more peace in the world.

The people of Old stated that good manner, right behavior and charity begin at home. If our leaders are doing the right thing and thinking right, looking for peace for themselves and for the people of their nation, along with keeping the peace of the world in mind, the world would have been much better than how it is today.

If the nation's leaders plan how to help under developed nations, developing nations, nations with no food and nations with diseases instead of fighting war against each other, the world would have been better than how it is today. The money used to

Three Solutions for World Peace

fight war because of a piece of land between nations would have helped to heal all the diseases that plague many people in other nations. It would have helped to bring water to the people in other nations where there is no water. The money would have given some nations the resources to have clean energy; it would have helped the research of all the deadly diseases such as cancer, the disease of Lupus, Sickle Cell Anemia, Leukemia and HIV. The money would have helped farmers to have more crops in the farm.

The Lord says, "Be fruitful and multiply and fill the Earth." He did not say to fight and kill each other. If the political leaders of the nations of the world plan and communicate in one accord, the world would have been much at peace and we would be able to care more for those who are in disaster such as tsunamis, earthquakes, volcanoes and hurricanes; instead of providing aid by spending money on wars, the world would have been better if these things were done. If those who have money help and live in peace without getting into what does not concern them, the world would have been better than how it is today. If everybody on this planet Earth would live and let others live, the world would have been a better place than how it is today. Let us live in peace and look for the peace of all people in the entire world.

Chapter One

Analysis of World Peace

On this special Wednesday I took a long walk around the city. As I walked, I began to think about all that has been going on around the world in all the nations. I came to the realization in a clear and precise manner that we are in need of peace in all the nations of the Earth.

Therefore, I have researched the subject by looking back as far as twenty years ago. I looked at all the nations and parts of the world that are riddled with violence, that are constantly going through terrorist actions, suicide bombings, experiencing political oppression and unrest with many killings.

I thought to myself, what are we going to do to stop all these violent, hatred, evils that plague the people of the world? I decided to find out what are all the religions of the world doing

Three Solutions for World Peace

about world peace. What are they doing or trying to do to solve the problems that are going on in the world? What are they doing or trying to do in other countries to make our world peaceful, comfortable and safer. I thought to myself-what if all the young college graduate students control or entered the political system? Would that change the world and create peace? What if all women are in the political system and controlling the world, would that bring about peace? I said to myself- what if all men control the political system? Would they bring peace to all the nations in the world?

As I walk, I continue to think, what is it that we need to do or introduce to the people in all the nations that can change the world and bring peace to the people in all the nations. What is it that the world needs? I found out that violence and killing are more in the countries where there is oil and money. There is more killing and more violence in these countries than in some poor nations.

I decided to look at the role of all the religions in regards to world peace. I decided to do some review of all the religions of the world. What do they say? What do they have in common? What is their interpretation of peace in their prayer? Do they pray for peace in their prayers and meditation according to their religion? What do they say about world peace and how do they pray? What are their views and perspective about world peace? What are the concerns they have towards peace of the Earth?

Three Solutions for World Peace

Chapter Two

Baha'i Religion Prayer for World Peace

I started with Baha'i Religion. According to the history in the Baha'i Holy Book, the Baha'i faith was founded a century and half ago. Baha'i faith is among the world religions. Its global scope is mirrored in the composition of its membership, representing many sections of humanity. Baha'i faith comes from every nation, ethnic and trial groups, cultures, professions, and many social economic classes.

The founder was Bahá'u'lláh, a Persian noble man from Teheran, who in the mid- nineteenth century left a life of princely comfort and security and, in the face of intense persecution and deprivation, brought to humanity a stirring new message of peace and unity. He claimed to be a messenger from God. His life, work and influences parallel to that of Abraham, Krishna, Moses,

Zoroaster, Buddha, Christ and Mohammad. The Baha'i religion according to the view of its founder, Bahá'ulláh, has the most succession of divine messenger of God.

He taught unity. He taught that there is only one God and only one human race. All of humanity is one family and men and women are equal as well. He taught that all prejudice, racial, religious, national or economic discrimination is destructive and must be overcome. Bahá'ulláh gave special attention to the problem of prejudice. At the heart of his message is a call for mutual understanding and fellowship among the nations, cultures and peoples. He believed that there was only one human race and that one must not be prejudice against another in any way to include race, ethnicity, nationality, religion or social background.

His teachings provided that one must overcome all prejudice if humanity is to create a peaceful and just global society. The unity of religion and science, including economic problems, is linked to spiritual problems. There is one God and all major religions come from God.

The oneness of religion and world peace is the crying need of our time. The religion believes in the promise of world peace. The belief that life should be seen as an eternal process of joyous spiritual discovery and growth, according to the Baha'i teachings, the true nature of human beings are spiritual. Beyond the physical, each human being has a rational soul, created by God. Baha'i believed that the seeker must at all times put his trust in God, must renounce the peoples of the Earth, must detach himself from the world and dust and cleave unto Him who is the Lord of lords.

He believed that all the world religions represent stages in the revelation of God's will and purpose for humanity. "The Earth is one country, mankind its citizens." Upon reviewing the type of religion that combined all other religions of the world and believed that the world should be assessed as one country and every inhabitant human being should be viewed as a citizen. Bahia's believed the crucial need facing humanity is to find a unifying vision of the nature and purpose of life and of the future of society. Such a vision unfolds in the writings of Bahá'ulláh. *The Baha'i prayer for peace is,* "Be generous in prosperity and thankful in adversity. Be fair in thy judgment and guarded in thy speech. Be a lamp unto those who walk in darkness and a home to the stranger. Be eyes to the blind and a guiding light unto the feet of the erring. Be a breath of life to the body of humankind, dew to the soil of the human heart and a fruit upon the tree of humility."

In reviewing this prayer, I found out that it does not mention peace or any solution to world peace. It is a good prayer mentioning thankfulness, generosity in prosperity and thankfulness to all the adversity that happens around us, a lamp to those who walk in darkness, an eye to the blind, but the prayer left one important thing that the world needed-peace. This religion still does not mention anywhere to solve the world violence and wars. The religion does not have anything to offer in terms of solving world peace because the religion missed an important aspect of what could bring world peace or how to achieve world peace.

Chapter Three

Shinto Religion Prayer for World Peace

I decided to move forward and review another religion called "Shinto." Shinto is the indigenous faith of the Japanese people. It is as old as Japan itself. It is an ethnic religion, which has continued from ancient times in Japan to the present. It permeates all aspects of the life and culture of the Japanese people, and moreover, it has the power to accept foreign culture and transform it into something Japanese. In origin it is a complex of ancient folk belief and rituals and is basically animistic religion that perceives the presence of deities or of the sacred in animals, in plants and even in things which have no life, such as rocks and waterfalls.

Its roots go back to the distant past. A large number of artifacts discovered at sites dating from the Jomon period, said to have been founded in about 300 BC. In early Japan, seasonal festivals observed various regions, ancestral cults and reverence towards supernatural forces were linked with legends of the creation of the Japanese islands and the descent of deities to populate them. Shinto appears to be a Japanese form of religious practice which enjoyed close ties with people's everyday lives in the past and continues to do so to the present day. Shinto has no founder and no scripture corresponding to the Bible of Christianity or the Qur'an of Islam. It does not have an organized or systematized religious community. Therefore, it has been said by some that Shinto is not a religion. Shinto remains to be Japans' major religion. It is the native religion of Japan and was once its state religion.

Shinto is a religion of Japan marked by a great reverence of nature, ancestors and emperors. Shintoism Kami is another name for the Shinto religion. Kami is the Japanese word for the spirit's natural forces, or essence, in the faith. Although the word is sometimes translated as "god" or "deity", some Shinto believers argued that such a translation can be misunderstood or misleading. The usage of the word can be compared to the Sanskrit "Deva" and the Hebrew "Elohim", which also refer to God, or spirits. Shinto does not have a founder and does not have sacred scriptures like the Bible. Shinto is deeply rooted in the Japanese people and traditions.

"Shinto gods" are called Kami. They are sacred spirits, which takes the form of things and concepts important to life, such as wind, rain, mountains, trees, rivers and fertility. Humans become Kami after they die and are revered by their families as ancestral Kami. The Kami of extraordinary people are even enshrined at some shrines. Shinto Priests perform Shinto rituals and often live on the Shrine grounds. Men and women were allowed to be priests, marry and have children. *The Shinto prayer for peace is,* "Although the people living across the ocean surrounding us, I believe, are all our brothers and sisters, why are there constant troubles in this world? Why do winds and waves rise in the ocean surrounding us? I only earnestly wish that the wind will soon puff away all the clouds which are hanging over the tops of the mountains."

After reviewing this prayer for world peace, I found out that it only talks about the people that surrounded us across the ocean and asks questions why there are constant troubles in the world. They want to know why wind and waves rise in the oceans; it does not mention any prayer or solution for world peace.

Three Solutions for World Peace

Chapter Four

Sikh Religion Prayer for World Peace

The basis of this religion is the union of soul with God. A Sikh disciplines his thoughts and actions so that the five obstacles such as lust, anger, greed, materialism and ego are dispelled and the soul will be able to be united with God. Sikhs believe that the cycle of reincarnation is escaped by this union. Guru, Nanak, was the founder of Sikhism. He was born in 1409. He preached a message of love and understanding. He criticized the blind rituals of the Hindus and Muslims. Sikh is a religion that originated in India during the 16th century and is related both to Hinduism and Islam. He established the Khalsa order: meaning the pure, soldier-saints, virtues of commitment, dedication and social conscious.

Guru Nanak summed the basis of Sikh lifestyles such as Naam Japo, KiratKami and Wand Kay Shako, which means they meditate on the holy name "Wahaguru." They work diligently and honestly and share one's and each other's fruits and foods. They believe that there is one supreme eternal reality, the truth, the immanent in all things, creator of all things, immanent in creation. Sikhism is a religion today with a following of over 20 million people worldwide and is ranked as the world's 5th largest religion.

Sikhism preaches a message of devotion and remembrance of God at all times, truthful living, equality of mankind and denounces superstitions and blind rituals. Sikhism is open to all through the teachings of its 10 Gurus enshrined in the Sikh Holy Book and living guru, Sri Guru granth Sahib. In Sikhism one's personal dedication to living a good life is important, but another important aspect of Sikhism is the Sangat. Without fear and hatred, beyond birth and death, self-revealing, which is known by the Guru's grace. Sikhs are required to stay away from the world of sin and any nature of sin. They live a life of a householder, which means selfless service; this is an integral part of Sikh worship that is very easily observed. Visitors of any religion or socio-economic background are welcome, they serve people of all origins while sitting together on the same level on the floor. Sikh's protect the religious and political rights of all people and prevents discrimination, which is an integral part of the Sikh faith. Sikhism a progressive religion well ahead of its time when it was founded over 500 years ago. The Sikh religion today has a 20 million people following worldwide and is ranked as the world's 5th largest religion.

Sikhism claims that there is only one God. He is the same and for all people of all religions. They believe that the soul goes through cycles of births and deaths before it reaches the human form. They believe that the goal of life is to lead an exemplary existence so that one may merge with God. Sikhs remember God at all times and practice living a virtuous and truthful life while maintaining a balance between their spiritual obligations and temporal obligations. The true path to achieving salvation and merging with God does not require renunciation of the world or celibacy, but living the life of a householder, earning an honest living and avoiding worldly temptations and sins. Sikhism condemns blind rituals such as fasting, visiting places of pilgrimage, superstitions, worship of the dead and idol worship. Sikhism preaches that people of different races, religions, or sex are all equal in the eyes of God. It teaches the full equality of men and women. Women can participate in any religious function or perform any Sikh ceremony or lead the congregation in prayer.

I turned to a Sikh prayer for peace, "God Judges us according to our deeds, not the coat that we wear. Truth is above everything, but higher still is truthful living. Know that we attain

God when we love and only that victory endures in consequence of which no one is defected." The prayer is good, but there is no mention of world peace in their prayer. Therefore, in my own view they don't have solution to world peace.

Chapter Five

Hindus Religion Prayer for World Peace

Hinduism has grown and become the world's third largest religion among Christianity and Islam. Followers are over 950 million, which is about fourteen percent of the world population. It is the religion of India, Nepal and Tamils in Sri Lanka. The Hindu religion is traditionally among the world's most religiously tolerant faiths. The Hindu religion is regarded as the world's oldest organized religion.

Hindu's worship recognizes a single deity, a single founder, a specific theological system, a single concept of deity, a single holy text, a single system of morality, a central religious authority and a single concept of a prophet. They view other gods and goddesses as manifestations of the supreme God.

Three Solutions for World Peace

I will move forward to Hindus Religion. Hinduism is the chief religion of India. The religion is based upon the worship of Brahma, but recognizes many other gods and goddesses, that also includes various schools of philosophy and a system of social organization and customs. Hinduism is generally regarded as the world's oldest organized religion. It consists of thousands of different religious groups that have evolved in India since 1500 BCE. Because of the wide variety of Hindus traditions, freedom of beliefs and practices are notable features of Hinduism. Most forms of Hinduism are henotheistic religions. They recognize a single deity and view other Gods and Goddesses as manifestations or aspects of that supreme God. Henotheistic and polytheistic religions have traditionally been among the world's most religiously tolerant faiths. As a result, India has traditionally been one of the most religiously tolerant in the world.

Hinduism has grown to become the world's third largest religion after Christianity and Islam. The origins of Hinduism traces the religion's roots to the Indus Valley civilization (circa 4000 to 2200) was influenced by many invasions over thousands of years. The major influences occurred when light-skinned, nomadic "Aryan" Indo-European tribes invaded Northern India (circa 1500 BCE) from the steppes of Russia and Central Asia. Hinduism has been viewed in the West as a polytheistic religion, one that worships multiple deities, gods and beliefs. This is not particularly accurate. It is also viewed as a monotheistic religion because it recognizes only one supreme God. Hinduism is Trinitarian because Brahman is simultaneously visualized as a triad-one God with three persons. Brahma is the Creator, who is continuing to create new realities and Vishnu, the preserver, who preserves these new creations. Whenever Brahma's eternal order is threatened, Vishnu travels from Heaven to Earth in one of ten incarnations. Shiva, the Destroyer, is at times compassionate, erotic and destructive.

The earliest Hindu Scriptures are henotheistic; they recognize multiple male and female deities, but recognize one as supreme. Hinduism viewed as native of all the inhabitants of India whose religion is Hinduism. *The Hindu's prayer of peace is*, "Oh God, lead us from the unreal to the real. Oh God, lead us from darkness to light. Oh God, lead us from death to immortality. Shanti (Peace) unto all. Oh Lord God almighty, may there be peace in celestial regions. May there be peace on Earth. May the waters be appeasing. May herbs be wholesome and may trees and plants bring peace to all. May all beneficent beings bring peace to us. May the Vedic (Sanskrit, Vedas) law propagate peace all through the world. May all things be a source of peace to us. And may thy peace itself bestow peace on all and many that peace comes to me also."

This prayer for world peace, mentions the name of God, the prayer makes an attribute to God's power and calls for peace in the world. "May there be peace on Earth." The prayer calls for God's leading from unreal things to the real things, from darkness into light. This is a very good prayer because the entire world is full of darkness. Ninety-five percent of the light of God would bring peace to the world, if people of the world work towards light and if their work and life are full of light. People that stay in darkness are full of evil and hatred. Darkness and light cannot work together. Wherever darkness is, when the light gets there, darkness disappears. It is a very good prayer that God should lead the people of the world from darkness to light. Still the prayer does not mention a solution to world peace. Therefore, the journey continues in search of the solution for world peace.

Chapter Six

Buddhism Religion Prayer for World Peace

Now I turn to the Buddhism religion. Buddhist's believe in Buddhism. This is a great Asiatic religion founded by Gautama Buddha in the sixth century, B. C. Two of the basic beliefs of Buddhism are the principles of rebirth and karma. There now follows a brief introduction to these topics taken from Geshe Kelsang's book, "Eight Steps to Happiness." Buddhist's believe the mind is neither physical, nor a by-product of purely physical processes, but a formless continuum that is a separate entity from the body. When the body disintegrates at death, the mind does not cease. Although our superficial conscious mind ceases, it does so by dissolving into a deeper level of consciousness, called the very subtle mind. The continuum of our very subtle mind has no beginning and no end, and it is this mind which, when completely purified, transforms into the omniscient mind of a Buddha. Every action we perform leaves an imprint, or potential, on our very subtle mind, and each karmic potential eventually gives rise to its own effect. Buddhist's believe that our mind is like a field and performing actions, is like sowing seeds in that field. Positive or virtuous actions sow the seeds of future happiness and negative or non-virtuous actions, sow the seeds of future suffering. This definite relationship between actions and their effect-virtue causing happiness and non-virtue causing suffering is known as the law of karma. An understanding of the law of karma is the basis of Buddhist morality.

Buddhism is a religion and philosophy indigenous to the Indian sub-continent and encompasses a variety of traditions, beliefs and practices, largely based on the teaching attributed to Siddhartha Gautama, who is commonly known as the Buddha. The Buddha lived and taught in the eastern part of India subcontinent sometime between the 6th and 4th centuries BCE.

Buddhists recognize him as an awakened or enlightened teacher who shares his insights to help sentient beings and ignorance craving and suffering of dependent origination realize and attain nirvana. Two major branches of Buddhism are recognized. The Theravada and Mahayana Theravada have a widespread following in Sri Lanka and Southeast Asia. Mahayana is found throughout East Asia and includes the traditions of pure land Zen Buddhism, Nichiren Buddhist, Tibetan Buddhism, Shingon Buddhism, Tiantai Buddhism, Tendai Buddhism and Shinnyoen Buddhism. In some classifications, the Vajrayana practice mainly in Tibet and Mongolia and adjacent parts of China and Russia are recognized as a third branch, while others classify it as a part of Mahayana. While Buddhism remains most popular within Asia, both branches are now found throughout the world. Estimates of Buddhists worldwide vary significantly, depending on the way Buddhist adherence is defined. Lower estimates of Buddhism are between 530-500 million.

There are around 350 million Buddhists and a growing number of them are Westerners. They follow many different forms of Buddhism, but all traditions are characterized by nonviolence, lack of dogma, tolerance of differences and usually by the practice of meditation. Taught by qualified Western teachers, the meditations are very easy to understand and apply to our daily lives. The classes are suitable for both beginners and more advanced meditation practitioners and emphasize how to meditate and practice in our New York urban environment.

Meditation is a simple, yet profound method to improve the quality of our lives and develop inner peace. Through following very simple, practical instructions we can learn to let go of the causes of our pain and dissatisfaction and gain the inner peace and clarity we seek. They offer a wide range of classes from basic introductions to Buddhist meditation, to applying Buddha's teachings to daily life issues such as anger and improving relationships, as well as providing comprehensive study programs of the Buddhist view, meditation and action.

Buddhism is a path of practice and spiritual development leading to insight into the true nature of life. Buddhist practices, such as meditation, are means of changing oneself in order to develop the qualities of awareness, kindness and wisdom. The experience developed within the Buddhist tradition over thousands of years has created an incomparable resource for all those who wish to follow a path - a path which ultimately culminates in enlightenment or Buddhahood. Because Buddhism does not include the idea of worshipping a creator God, some people do not see it as a religion in the normal, Western sense. The basic tenets of the Buddhist teaching are straightforward and practical: nothing is fixed or permanent; actions have consequences; change is possible. Thus Buddhism addresses itself to all people irrespective of race, nationality or gender. It teaches practical methods (such as meditation) which enable people to realize and utilize its teachings in order to transform their experience to be fully responsible for their lives and to develop the qualities of wisdom and compassion.

The Buddhist religion believes that after we die our very subtle mind leaves our body and enters the intermediate state, or "bardo" in Tibetan. It teaches the eight-fold path of right belief, right resolve, right word, right act, right life, right effort, right thinking and right meditation. *The Buddhist prayer for world peace is*, "May all beings everywhere plagued with sufferings of body and mind quickly be freed from their illnesses. May those frightened cease to be afraid and may those bound be free. May the powerless find power and may people think of being friendly to one another. May those who find themselves in trackless fearful wildernesses, the children, the aged, and the unprotected be guarded by beneficent celestials and may they swiftly attain Buddha-hood."

This is another prayer that is directed to other things, but not to the peace of the world. The prayer mentions so many things such as fearfulness, unprotected, guarded by beneficent and celestials, but it did not mention world peace. The concept of world peace to the Buddhist is very different from what is going on in the world. I decided to look into other world religion.

Three Solutions for World Peace

Chapter Seven

Zoroastrian Religion Prayer for World Peace

The Zoroastrian Religion is defined as one of the oldest religions in the world. It is definitely one of the first monotheist religions. It was founded by Zoroaster and it believes in one God, Ahura Mazda. There are very few Zoroastrians in the world today, but it still holds an important place. A large part of their population is divided between Iran and India. The Zoroastrians living in India are called Parsis. Its disciples of Zoroaster or followers of Zoroastrianism: The religion was founded by Zoroaster in Persia around 1000 B.C. Zoroastrianism believes in one god, Ahura Mazda, who is omniscient, omnipotent, omnipresent, impossible for a normal human being to conceive, unchanging, the creator of everything and the source of all the goodness and happiness in the world. It's a religious system that is based on the belief that there are two creative powers, good and evil, and that the good would triumph over evil in life after death.

Zoroastrianism is a religion and philosophy based on the teachings of Prophet Zoroaster and was formerly among the world's largest religions. It was probably founded some time before the 6th century BCE in greater Iran. Zoroastrianism, the creator Ahuro Mazda, is all good and no evil originates from Him. Thus, in Zoroastrianism, there is belief that good and evil have a distinct source, with evil trying to destroy the creation of Mazda and good trying to sustain it. Mazda is not immanent in the world. His creation is represented by the Amesha Spentas and the host of other Yazatas, through whom the works of God are evident to humanity, and through whom worship of Mazda is ultimately directed.

The most important texts of the religion are those of the Avesta, of which a significant portion has been lost, and mostly only the liturgies of which have survived. The lost portions are known of only through references and brief quotations in the later works, primarily from the 9th to 11th centuries. It was a state religion of a significant portion of the Iranian people for many centuries. After which, it collapsed and disintegrated into what was gradually marginalized by Islam from the 7th century onwards with the decline of the Sassanid Empire.

The basic beliefs are that there is one universal and transcendent God, Ahura Mazda. His is the uncreated Creator to whom all worship is ultimately directed. Ahura Mazda's creation and evident as asha truth and order is the antithesis of chaos, which is evident as druj, falsehood and disorder. The resulting conflict involves the entire universe, including humanity, which has an active role to play in the conflict. The religion states that active participation in life through good thoughts, good words, and good deeds is necessary to ensure happiness and to keep chaos at bay. This active participation is a central element in Zoroaster's concept of freewill; therefore, all forms of monasticism are rejected.

Zoroastrianism holds the belief that water and fire are the agents of ritual purity. The associated purification ceremonies are considered the basis of ritual life. Fire is considered a medium through which spiritual insight and wisdom is gained and water is considered the source of that wisdom. Zoroastrian's believe that life is a temporary state in which a mortal is expected to actively participate in the continuing battle between truth and falsehood.

Prior to being born, the soul of an individual is still united with its fravashi; of which there are very many, and which have existed since Mazda created in universe. During life, the fravashi acts as guardian and protector. The creator interacts with the world. On the fourth day after death, the dead will be revived and the soul is reunited with its fravashi, in which the experiences of life in the material world are collected for continuing battle in the spiritual world; they do not have a notion of reincarnation, not until the final renovation of the world. The religion strongly encourages followers to marry others of the same faith, but this is not a requirement of the religion itself. This supreme God is worshipped and his prophet is Zoroaster. Zoroaster is not worshipped, but is followed as his directed path of truth and righteousness; asha will lead men and women to God. Zoroastrians are not fire worshippers as is generally believed. Fire is an important symbol in their faith. *The Zoroastrian prayer for world peace is,* "We pray to God to eradicate all the misery in the world, that understanding triumph over ignorance, that generosity triumph over contempt and that truth triumph over falsehood."

This is a good prayer that Zoroastrianism's pray that God should eradicate all the miseries in the world and ask for understanding to be triumphant over ignorance. There is mention of generosity, contempt, truth and falsehood. All these are the causes of so many miseries in the world. The prayer does not mention any solution for the world peace. I decided to explore another religion.

Chapter Eight

Jainism Religion Prayer for World Peace

According to the world religion books, Jainism is an Indian religion that prescribes a path of non-violence towards all living beings. Its beliefs and practices emphasize the necessity of self–effort, which move the soul towards divine consciousness and liberation. Souls that overcome it's own inner enemies and achieve the state of Supreme Being are called a "Jina" or "Victor." The ultimate status of these perfect souls is called "Siddha." Jainism is also referred to as "Shramana", which means "self-reliant" or "path of the nigathas", which means, "people with no attachments." The doctrine teaches that Jainism always existed and will always exist, although historically the foundation of the organized or present forms of Jainism to some times between the 9th and 6th century BC. Jainism has its roots in the Indus Valley Civilization, which reflected native spirituality before the Indo-Aryan migration into India.

Jainism is a small, but influential religious minority with as many as 6 million followers in India and continues growing in North America, Western Europe and Australia, etc. The Jainism religion has influence and contributed to ethical, political and economic lives in India. Jainism is an ancient tradition and has the highest degree of literacy for a religious community in India. The belief is that every living being has a soul, every soul is divine with innate qualities of infinite knowledge, perception, power and bliss, therefore they regard every living being as you do yourself, harming no one and being kind to all living beings. They believe that every soul is born as a heavenly being, human, sub-human or hellish being according to its own karma; every soul is the architect of its own life, here or hereafter. They also believe that when the soul is freed from karmas, it becomes free and attains divine consciousness, experiencing infinite knowledge, perception, power and the bliss, which means Moksha's Jainism religion.

They believe in the three rights-right view, right knowledge and right conduct, which provide the way to this realization. They believe that there is no supreme divine creator, owner, preserver or destroyer. The universe is self-regulated. And every soul has the potential to achieve divine consciousness through its own efforts. The Jainism religion believe in non-violence, to be soul consciousness rather than body consciousness. The foundation of right view, the condition of right knowledge and the kernel of right conduct leads to a state of being unattached to worldly things, being non-judgmental and non-violent. This includes compassion and forgiveness in thoughts, words and actions towards all living beings and respecting the views of others, which means non-absolutism.

The Jainism religion stresses the importance of controlling the senses including the mind, as they can drag one far away from true nature of the soul. Jainism put limitation on possessions and led a life that is useful to self and others. Attachment to an object is possessiveness and non-possessiveness is the balancing of needs and desires while staying detached from worldly possessions. Jainism religion stresses the importance of controlling the senses including the mind, as they can drag one far away from true nature of other soul. One is recommended to enjoy the company of the holy and better-qualified people, to be merciful to afflicted souls and tolerate the perverse incline. Jainism believed that four things are very difficult for a soul to attain: human birth, knowledge of the laws governing the souls, absolute conviction in the philosophy of non- violence and practicing this knowledge with conviction in day-to-day life activities. They believed that human life should not be wasted in an evil ways; they must rise on the ladder to spiritual evolution. The goal of Jainism religion is the liberation of the soul from the negative effects of unenlightened thoughts, speech, and action.

This goal is achieved through the clearance of karmic obstructions by the following the triple gems of Jainism, which are right view, right knowledge and right conduct. They believed in honoring Jainism teachers and all the monks and nuns by saluting them in a proper way. They receive inspiration from them to follow their path to achieve true bliss, they worship the icons of jinas, arihants and Tirthankaras, who have conquered their inner passions and attained divine consciousness with and through the study of the Jainism's Scriptures of these liberated people.

Jainism's fundamental prayer can be recited at any time of the day; they pray by reciting this Namokar mantra. The devotee bows in respect to liberated souls still in human form, which means arihants-fully liberated souls forever free from rebirth, which means siddhas. They also bow to the spiritual leaders, which means Acharyas teachers that include all the monks and nuns. Jainism acknowledges the existence of powerful heavenly souls that look after the well being of Tirthankaras, usually found in pairs, around the icons as male and female guardian deities. Deities that have supernatural power are souls wandering through the cycles of births and deaths, just like most other souls, which some people also worship.

Jainism is an Indian religion that prescribes a path of non-violence towards all living beings. Its philosophy and practice emphasize the necessity of self-effort to move the soul towards divine consciousness and liberation, although historians date the foundation of organized or present form of Jainism to some time between the 9th and 6th century B. C. Jainism is an ancient religion from India that teaches that the way to liberation and bliss is to live a life of harmlessness and renunciation. The aim of the Jainism life is to achieve liberation of the soul.

The Jainism prayer for world peace is, "Peace and universal love is the essence of the gospel preached by all the enlightened ones. The Lord has preached that equanimity is the Dharma. I forgive all creatures, and may all creatures forgive me. Unto all have I amity, and unto none, enmity. Know that violence is the root cause of all miseries in the world violence in fact is the knot of bondage. "Do not injure any living being." This is the eternal, perennial and unalterable way of spiritual life. A weapon, however powerful it may be, can always be superseded by a superior one; but no weapon can be superior to nonviolence and love.

This prayer does not suggest any solution for world peace. It did mentioned forgiveness to all the creatures; it also mentioned all the violence and bondage with the giving of instructions to not injure any living being. Why is it that violence is higher in some countries with religious conflicts than other countries without religious conflict? There is no mention of world peace in this prayer and there is no suggested solution for the world peace. The Jainism religion preaches non-violence and love, but still there is much violence going on within the people that affect the country and the world. They were unable to solve the problems of the world of daily violence around them and in the entire world. Jainism religion continues to preach non-violence and love, but nobody and no one listens. Therefore, the search for solution to world peace continues.

Chapter Nine

Native American Religion Prayer for World Peace

Now we are going to take a look at Native American religions. Native American beliefs are deeply rooted in their culture. Native American religions exhibit a great deal of diversity, largely due to the relative isolation of different tribes that were spread out across the entire North American Continent for thousands of years, allowing different beliefs and practices between tribes. The Native American religion is closely connected to the land in which the Native Americans dwelt and the supernatural. Native American religious practice an omnipresent, invisible universal force, pertaining to the "three life crises of birth, puberty, death, spirits and visions." The Native American religions tend not to be institutionalized, but experiential and personal.

Native American spirituality is often characterized by animism or panentheism with a strong emphasis on the importance of personal spirituality and its inter-connectivity with one's own day-to-day life and a deep connection between the natural and spiritual worlds.

The Native American religion is characterized as a personal religion. Individual asceticism through sweat lodge ceremonies and other rituals that appear to resemble idol worship makes the understanding of the faith and religion problematic.

Most important to understand is that Native American religions carried out mainly in a family, or tribal location first and are better explained as more of a process or journey other than a religion.

The Native American religion emphasized relationship experience between Creator and created being; the relationship with God is experienced as a relationship with all of creation, which interestingly enough is ever present and does not require an institution or building. The Native American religion believes that all of creation has life. Including rocks, tries, mountains and everything that is visible in life lives. All are part of creation and therefore, life must be respected. The Native American religion belief is that God is an intrinsic dimension of all their relations.

God is known indirectly through an awareness of the relationships or links between various aspect of both the physical and the supernatural realms. Spirituality makes no distinction between the realms, which is the living and the dead, visible and invisible, past and present, Heaven and the Earth. The Native American religion has never seen their spiritual beliefs and practices as a religion; rather they see their culture and social structure as infused with spirituality, which is an integral part of their lives and culture.

The history of American religions is dominated by the presence of Christianity brought to the New World by European settlers. Columbus' discovery in 1492 marked the beginning of a massive "white" invasion that would consume the entire continent of North America over the next four centuries. Although Christianity manifested itself in countless denominations, it was, nevertheless, the umbrella under which most Europeans in America gathered. It served as common ground on which white settlers could stand together in the struggle for survival in the wilderness of the New World.

Whatever differences there were between denominations were insignificant when compared to the differences between the White European Christianity and their counterparts on the continent, the resident Native Americans. This fact, along with the desire and need for land, turned Native Americans into a convenient enemy for most groups of European settlers.

In essence, time had run out for the indigenous race that populated the continent of North America. Like the Israelites of the sixth century B.C.E., Native Americans were faced with an enemy that was more advanced. Ironically, the invading Whites are the religious descendants of those same Israelites who were conquered by the Babylonians in 586 B.C.E.

Armed with technologically advanced weapons, diseases, which were foreign to the continent and a concept known as "Manifest Destiny", European settlers began an assault on the North American Continent. The result of which was nothing short of genocide. Within four hundred years of their first contact, the White man had succeeded in stripping Native American civilizations of virtually all of their land and had nearly wiped their cultures from the face of the Earth.

Popular American history has traditionally viewed the past through White's eyes. Much of the history and culture of many Native American civilizations were lost during the European invasion of the continent. The absence of a written language among most tribes force them to depend on aril traditions that were difficult to maintain as their civilizations were being killed off and separated by the dominant White culture.

For this reason, it is often difficult to locate information concerning the religious beliefs and rituals of the large variety of Native American civilizations that flourished in North America before the time of the European invasion.

This project will provide some of this information by taking a cross-section of certain Native American tribes from separate and distinct geographic regions and comparing certain aspects of each of their religious beliefs and rituals. I plan to show how each tribe's religion was impacted by the environmental conditions that surrounded it and to show in what ways these religions were affected by the invasion of Christianity.

The Iroquois Nation of the Eastern woodlands, the Dakota tribes of the central plains, and the Apache tribes of the Southwestern desert shall serve as the subjects of this project.

While the Iroquois belief system centered on the idea of a benevolent Great Spirit, it did not ignore the existence of evil in the world. Evil is represented by the brother of the Great Spirit, "Ha-ne-go-ate-geh", or "the Evil-Minded" (1954, 147). This evil spirit exists independently and controls its own inferior spiritual beings. These agents of evil also exist in the material world and are placed there in an attempt to bring about evil. According to Morgan, the Great Spirit does not have any type of positive authority over the Evil-Minded, except for the power to overcome him when necessary (1954, 148). The red race is left to choose either obedience to the Great Spirit or submission to the Evil-Minded. It is important to note that the Iroquois developed the idea of an immortal soul. This soul was judged by the Great Spirit upon the death of the body. The threat of punishment in the afterlife increased morality concerns, which aided in the success of the Iroquois Nation.

The ritual ceremonies practiced by the Iroquois tribes were systematic worship services that occurred in accordance to certain seasonal periods throughout the year. The rituals were handed down through the generations and remained unchanged for centuries. Festivals most commonly occurred during important agricultural periods. Worship and thanks were given to the Great Spirit for protection and survival. One of the "Invisible Agents" was usually honored depending on what time of year the ceremony was taking place. The ceremonies were led by "Keepers of the Faith", or "Ho-nun-den-ont" (Morgan 1953, 177). They were not an organized priesthood like one would imagine, but rather a loosely organized council of qualified individuals who were assigned the task of maintaining the ritual practices of the Iroquois people.

The belief system of the Iroquois was the closest a Native American civilization had come to the complex theology of Christianity. One major difference between the two religions is evident when looking at how each faith explains mankind's participation in the workings of the Universe. While most Christian denominations sought to participate actively in the evolution of their world, the Iroquois say mankind was too insignificant to take part in the grand scheme of the Great Spirit.

For example, many Christian denominations, like the Puritans of New England, believed that they were the chosen people of God and were working toward the creation of a true "Kingdom of God" located in America. The Iroquois, on the other hand, believed that the world was as it should be and there was nothing that could be done by mankind to change this fact. This idea would eventually change somewhat as the Iroquois were influenced more and more by European Christianity.

Furthermore, their ideas concerning punishment in the afterlife were also influenced by Christian concepts. According to Morgan, the Christian concept of purgatory seems to have seeped into the Iroquois belief system sometime during the White man's invasion (1954, 163).

While the Iroquois Nation was the strongest Native American civilization East of the Mississippi River, their integration into the dominant White culture went relatively smooth compared to most other instances of integration among the native tribes of North America. I believe this was due to the similarities between their belief systems, which made it easier for the two races to find common ground.

The religion practiced by the Iroquois descendants is remarkably similar to the one practiced by their ancestors. The similarities between the two distinct religions seem to have saved the weaker Native American system from extinction.

Native peoples worshiped an all-powerful, all-knowing creator or Master Spirit in forms of both genders. The Native American Religion also hosted lesser supernatural entities, including an evil god who dealt with the Earth, with disaster, suffering and death. Members or believer's tribes believed in the immortality of the human soul and the afterlife.

The Indian societies of North America hoped to enlist the aid of the supernatural in controlling the natural and social world; each tribe had its own set of religious observances devoted to that aim. Native Americans perceived that "material" and "spiritual" as a unified realm of being, plants, animals and humans partook of divinity through connection with "Guardian Spirits." The belief also allowed for a myriad of "supernatural" entities that imbued their "natural" kin with life and power. Native American's believed that native culture and religion should be valued. Their beliefs and practices form an integral and part of their being. They believe that everything is sacred, from the largest mountain to the smallest plant, to animals. They also believed to spiritually honor and respect their creator and their Mother Earth; they also believed that every living thing was in touch with themselves and everything around them. They believe that they are part of everything and everything is part of them; and they are all one.

The Native American Prayer for world peace is, "O great Spirit of our ancestors, we raise the pipe to you, to your messengers the four winds, and the Mother Earth who provides for your children. Give us the wisdom to teach our children to love, to respect, to be kind to each other so that they may grow with peace in mind, let us learn to share all the good things that you provide for us on this Earth."

This is another powerful prayer, but directed to the spirit of ancestors, messengers of the four winds, asking for the wisdom to teach their children. This prayer does not call for the peace of God in the world. It is the prayer of the ancestors that those people they left behind in the world will have peace and live in peace. There are ancestors that are praying day and night for world peace, but the people of the world are not hearing them or are unable to hear them because they directed their prayer to God. I continue to explore all other religions of the world.

Chapter Ten

Native African Religion Prayer for World Peace

Native African Prayer for world peace, "Almighty God, the Great Thumb, we cannot evade to tie any knot, the Roaring Thunder that splits mighty trees, the all-seeing Lord on high who sees even the foot prints of an antelope on a rock mass here on Earth, you are the one who does not hesitate to respond to our call. You are the corner stone of peace."

After reviewing the prayer of the Native African prayer for peace, which acknowledges God's attribute and power, the prayer mentions that God is the corner- stone of peace, but does not give a solution for world peace. Acknowledgement of God's power in the world is very important and that was what the Native African prayer offered. Therefore, my search continues.

I decided to walk to Fordham University. I picked up four books about Torah Judaism and three books on English translations of The Holy Qur'ans for the in-depth studies and understanding of these two great religions.

Chapter Eleven

Jewish Religion Prayer for World Peace

In the Jewish Religion, the God of Abraham is the Father of Judaism, Christianity and Islam. Judaism is one of the greatest religions and the beginning of all the religions of the world. God, the Creator, is the Father of Jews, Christians and Muslims. Judaism was among the first religions that taught a belief in one God and was the ancestor of Christianity. The tradition of thought, morality and culture also associated with this religion is the religion of the Jewish people.

The Book of Torah enjoins: "Love your neighbor as yourself," and in the same chapter of Leviticus, "You shall love the stranger; love the one with whom you identify, as well as the one who seems different from you. You yourselves were once strangers in the land of Egypt." You see him as different, but he is just like you. We were once ourselves slaves in Egypt, strangers in a strange land, immersed in idolatry. So, we look at the stranger and project upon him that which we fear might be most true about ourselves. But what we fear is this, it is the Torah's insight because it is true. We instinctively hate the other for reminding us of the defect, which is our own.

Jewish prayer and rituals, as a corrective to those indications, refer to the God who took the Jewish people out of Egypt, the God who created the heavens and the Earth. Remember who you are, remembering from your past and that you are also exceptional. The verse concludes, "I am your, 'both your God and the stranger's. You are not only united in your history; you and the strangers, who you want distance from the camp, have the same God. So be open minded to the stranger within.'" In the Book of Torah God tells the Jewish people again and again that He is the God of the stranger and He is their God.

GOD GAVE TEN COMMANDMENTS TO MOSES

God gave unto Moses when he had made an end of communing with him upon Mount Sinai, two tables of testimony, tables of stone, written with the finger of God that is by His will and power. It should be clear to us on this Earth that only God can write his law on the heart of men by his Spirit which he gave us. God writes his will in the fleshy tables of the heart. The two tables were designed to direct us in our daily lives and duty towards God and towards His people. The tables of Ten Commandments also called tables of testimony, because this written law testified both the will of God concerning His people and His goodness and will towards them. And God spake all these words, saying, "I am the Lord thy God, which have brought thee out of the land of Egypt, out of the house of bondage. You shall not have any other gods before me. You shall not make for yourself any carved image, or any likeness of anything that is in heaven above, or that is in the earth beneath, or that is in the water under the earth; you shall not bow down to them nor serve them. For I, the Lord your God, am a jealous God, visiting the iniquity of the fathers on the children to the third and fourth generations of those who hate me, but showing mercy to thousands, to those who love Me and keep My commandments. You shall not take the name of the Lord your God in vain, for the Lord will not hold him guiltless who takes His name in vain. Remember the Sabbath day, to keep it holy. Six days you shall labor and do all your work, but the seventh day is the Sabbath of the Lord your God. In it you shall do no work: you, nor your son, nor your daughter, nor your manservant, nor your maidservant, nor your cattle, nor your stranger who is within your gates. For in six days the Lord made the heavens and the earth, the sea, and all that is in them, and rested the seventh day. Therefore the Lord blessed the Sabbath day and hallowed it. Honor your father and your mother, that your days may be long upon the land which the Lord your God is giving you. You shall not murder. You shall not commit adultery. You shall not steal. You shall not bear false witness against your neighbor. You shall not covet your neighbor's house; you shall not covet your neighbor's wife, nor his manservant, nor his maidservant, nor his ox, nor his donkey, nor anything that is your neighbor's." (Exodus 20:2-17)

The Ten Commandments mean exactly what they are. It is quite amazing how many of these commandments are being broken, people do not pay attention to it on a regular basis, not only by the Israelites alone, but by Christians and all the people of other religions. We have to realize that each of these Ten Commandments was based on what God is expecting from humanity on this Earth. It also shows the love of God in His created beings. Ten Commandments was given to guide us in our moral laws and in our decisions; that we may keep ourselves clean, out of trouble with the government, friends and all the other people that are close to us especially, our neighbors. God, the Creator, knows the best way and simple way for us to live a peaceful life and maintain good harmony with ourselves and with other people in the world.

The Jewish prayer for world peace is, "Jewish people believed that this prayer for peace is the traditionally included in the Shabbat Saturday Service. A lovely prayer drawn as one of the most prayed prayer in Judaism. "May we see the day when war and bloodshed cease, when great peace will embrace the whole world? Then nation shall not threaten nation and humankind will not again not war for all who live on Earth shall realize we have not come into being to hate or destroy; we have come into being to praise, to labor and to love. Compassionate God bless all the leaders of all nations with the power of compassion fulfill the promise conveyed in scripture, "I will bring peace to the land, and you shall lie down and no one shall terrify you. I will rid the land of vicious beats and it shall not be ravage by war." (Leviticus 26:2) "Let love and justice flow like a mighty stream. "But let justice roll on like a river, righteousness like a never failing stream." (Amos 5:24) Let peace fill the Earth as the waters fill the sea. "Come, let us go to the mountain of the Lord that we may walk the paths of the most high, and we shall beat our swords, into plough shares and our spears into pruning hooks. Nation shall not lift up sword against nation; neither shall they learn war any more. And none shall be afraid, for the mouth of the Lord of Hosts has spoken." (Isaiah 2:2-3)

Jewish people still go through violence and war between its neighboring countries. This is an ongoing war since the establishment of the Jewish people when God returned them back

Three Solutions for World Peace

to their land through the God of Abraham's permissive order, which can never be changed and will not change until the end of the world when the God of Abraham, Isaac and Jacob creates a new Earth where all the righteous people will dwell. Many lives has been wasted, properties destroyed, historic properties, things from the beginning of creation of the world have been destroyed because of the war that has never ceased in Israel and its neighboring countries. Many people continue to die; they are murdered daily because of a piece of land. The most interesting thing that many people that have never traveled to Israel is that many people from the neighboring countries living in Israel are at peace. I tried to talk to about five people, both Palestinians and Israelis about the war. They said that they don't know why fighting still going on. They believed that it was all Political. Muslim's Mosques are in the city of Jerusalem. They call on the name of Allah on the Mosque bell for worship five-times a day. Palestine's living in Israel are very happy, just as other people in the world. But still the two nations continue wasting the lives because of a piece of land. I asked one Palestine store owner in the Old City Jerusalem if he can tell me one good thing that these two countries have done for each other? He said yes, and mentioned one important good that they are constantly doing for the other, which I will not mention in this book.

Three Solutions for World Peace

Furthermore, one of the leaders of another country pointing fingers to the nation of Israel saying, "Israel that you see today very soon you will not see it no more." He did not give the reason for his statement. For practically no reason this leader threatened another nation, forgetting that innocent children, young and old people are living in the nation of Israel. It shows clearly that this person is a fake Muslim, not a believer and he is too far from Allah, according to the Muslim religion; he is not following the Holy Qur'an's. Peace is not in his vocabulary. He is dwelling in abusive of power. This prayer of peace for the world was a powerful prayer that wants the war among us to cease, wants us to go to the mountain of the Lord, follow the path and that nation must not lift up sword against nation. The prayer mentioned so many things that God wants us to do in order to be able to attain world peace. People are not listening to the spoken words of God.

There seems to be no solution, which will stop the nations from lifting up their sword against each other. What is it that the nations need to do with each other that will make them stop lifting sword up against each other? It was mentioned by God Himself, but people never pay attention. War is still going on, violence still continues and there is no peace within the neighboring countries. The nations must do their own part and God will answer the prayer; there is always what we must do so that God will listen to our prayer and answer our prayers.

Chapter Twelve

Islam Religion Prayer for World Peace

Now I turn to the Islam religion. The Islam Religion is the world's second largest religion with followers of over one billion. People called "Muslims" make up one-fifth of humanity. The word "Islam" means "Submission to God." Therefore, "a Muslim is a person who strives to submit to God." The Islam religion was founded by Prophet Mohammad in 610 A. D. Mohammad was a trader when God called him through a vision that Angel Gabriel spoke to him and dictated the Qur'an to him. Prophet Mohammad, who is the founder of Islamic religion, came directly from descendants of Ishmael.

The Holy Qur'an and generally chosen by the congregation times of prayer are: Morning, Afternoon, Late Afternoon and Sunset and by Nightfall. These five different prayers, which contain verses from the Holy Qur'an, are prayed in the Arabic Language, especially if the prayer is for personal supplications. The Muslim religion prefers that all the worshipers must worship in the Mosque. They can pray anywhere in the office, factories, the market place, in the fields and in the universities; they offer their prayer at the particular time. Prayer to the Muslim is like foods that must be eaten at that particular time of the day. Praying five-times a day is part of their life.

Another important principle of Islam is that they believe that everything belongs to God. God gave wealth to human beings in trust; possessions are purified by setting aside a percentage for the poor and the needy or for some other programs. They believe that the more they give, the more they grow in their religion. Therefore, "Sakh" is a very important to an individual. A Muslim may also give in secret as they please "Sadaqah." Sadaquh means to voluntary give charity.

The following were stated in the Holy Qur'an: Five Pillars' of Islam are the foundation of Muslim life which consisted of (1) Faith "Kalima" or belief in the oneness of God and in the finality of the Prophet Mohammad; Muslim's believe strongly that God called Prophet Mohammad to be His Messenger, "There is none worthy of worship, except God and Mohammad, who is the messenger of God." (2) The establishment of daily prayers "Salat" which is five times a day. (3) They also believe in alms giving which is called "Zadat." This strong declaration of faith, which is called the "Shahadah", is a simple formula that all the faithful pronounced and proclaimed. Most importantly in regards to this declaration, is that it is based on beliefs that the only purpose of life is to serve and be obedient to God, which can only be achieved through the teaching and practices of Prophet Mohammad. "Salam" which also means the name of prayer is an obligatory duty that Muslim's must pray five-times a day and this prayer link or glue rather is a direct channel to God. "Salah" flow through the worshiper and God. There are no exercises of hierarchical authority and there are no priests. Prayers are taught and learned from people who know. "Even meeting your brother with a cheerful face is an act of charity. (Five pillars of Islam & Holy Qur'an 2:182)

Prophet Mohammad also said, "Charity is a necessity for every Muslim," he continues with saying , "If a Muslim lacks charity or having nothing good to give others, he must clear he or herself from doing evil." Muslim's also believe in fasting, which is called "Sawm." Every year in the month of Ramadan from dawn until sundown abstaining from food, drink and any intimate relationships with their spouses or boyfriends/girlfriends. Those who are sick, senior citizens, women who are menstruating, pregnant women or nursing mothers are automatically excluded and they can make it up before the end of that particular year. Children learn how to fast and are taught to observe prayers at the age of thirteen. Fasting to Muslim's is mainly a method of self-purification and self-restraint. The belief that by cutting oneself from worldly comforts, for a period of time, will help the person to focus on his or her purpose in life and help them be constantly alert and aware of the presence of God.

The Holy Qur'an stated that, "O you who believe fasting is prescribed for you as it was prescribed to those who are before you to learn self-restraint." (Qur'an 2:183) Muslim's also believe strongly in the Holy Pilgrimage "Hajj." The pilgrimage to Mekkah is an obligation for those who are physically and financially able to do so, more than 3 million people visit Mekkah every year from all the nations of the world. 'Hajj" begins in the twelfth month of the Islamic lunar year; which always takes place in the summer as well as Ramadan during the fall or winter time. They visit places such as: Abrahamic origin Kabah 7 times, several times to the Hill of Safa, Marwa as Hagar – Abraham's wife during her search for water for her son Ishmael, Arafat desert outside Malkeh to join in prayer for God's forgiveness, which they believe they must do before the day of judgment. Hajj closes with "Eid al-adha" which is usually celebrated with prayer.

Muslim's believe in the "Six Articles of Faith" which are: faith in the unity of God, faith in Angels, faith in the Prophets, faith in the Book of Revelation (The Bible, Turay, Torah, Zabir, Psalm, Angel, the Gospels and the Holy Qur'an), faith in the afterlife, faith in destiny and divine decree. The main basis of Islam is the belief in one and only Almighty God. Muslims believe that there is only one supreme God who creates and controls everything in the world. God is the Creator, the Sustainer, the Ruler and the Judge of all people. To all Muslims, "Allah" is the personal name used for the One Almighty God. The further recognized that a person who believes in the Creator comes to love Him, Trust Him, Hope in Him and fear Him and not to disappoint Him, the closer the Muslim comes to God. Muslim's maintains strict monotheism in faith and worship is the cornerstone of the faith.

They believe that as God is an unseen being, beyond our limited human perception, it is sometimes difficult for us to imagine His characteristics. The Holy Qur'an offers a full description of God by using many different attributes or names, which help human beings to understand the nature of God. Muslim's believe that Allah created unseen beings, including Angels. Angels were created out of light and they work tirelessly to minister in Allah's Kingdom. Angels carried out Allah's orders with full obedience (Qur'an 66:6). The Arabic word for Angel is "Malaka", which means helper or assistant.

Muslims believe in the prophets. All prophets are human beings who received divine revelations in order to be role models, teachers and advisers to Muslim people. Individual prophets have different spiritual strength and power. The Qur'an mentions more than thirty different biblical prophets; beginning from Adam, Noah, Abraham, Lot to Jonah and on to Moses, Aaron David, Solomon and Jesus. Their stories are mentioned in the Holy Qur'an in the teaching or as an inspiration to the people.

Muslims believe that God sent human prophets to proclaim His teachings throughout the world as well as deliver the actual words of Allah to the people. Muslims believe in the revelation of five divine books. The Book of Zabor – Psalms revealed to David, The Book of Towah –Torah revealed to Moses, the Book of Injeel – Gospels revealed to Jesus, The Book of Qur'an revealed to Mohammad, The Book of Suhuf – Scrolls revealed to Abraham.

Muslims believe in the Day of Judgment when the life of this world and all that is in it will come to an end the time and the appointed day they don't know. The day is called, "Youm al-Qry-ama", which means they day of reckoning that everyone on Earth will be raised for Judgment by Allah. They believe that Allah will judge individual persons according to his or her faith and good and bad works. The Day of Judgment is also called in the Holy Qur'an as the day of peace for the righteous and a day of despair for the evildoers. "On the Day of Judgment, He shall set up scales of Justice, so that not a soul will be dealt with unjustly in the least. And if there be the weight of even a mustard seed, He will bring it to account" (Qur'an 21:47).

Muslims believe in destiny and divine decree, which is the final article of faith which is called: destiny, divine decree, predestination, fate, or in Arabic "Al-Qadr." Al-Qadr means power and ability and also means God alone has the power and ability to know the destiny of every creature. Muslims believe that since Allah is the sustainer of all life, nothing happens, except by His will and with His full knowledge; therefore, everything that happens on Earth has been predetermined by God – Allah. They still believe in human beings free will to choose a course of action.

Muslims believe that Allah does not force people to do anything; they can choose to obey Him or disobey Him. Muslims believe that everything that happens in life takes place according to the will of Allah. "To Allah we belong and to Allah we will return" (Qur'an 2:156-157).

Three Solutions for World Peace

Mohammad said, "There is only one God and His name is Allah. Worship Him." Islam spread across the Earth. Muslims are in North and South America, Western Europe, Africa, the Middle East and Asia. Islam is particularly popular in the Eastern side of North Africa and Western side of Asia. All other Muslims are all over the world. The Islamic region is the most tolerant religion in the world. Muslims pray five-times a day. This means, five times of straight communication with God of Allah, bowing down before Him five-times a day.

This religion should be able to structure people, make them to be at peace at all times, make them to be joyful more than any other people of other religions of the world. Praying five-times a day should make people to tolerate so many things that can cause anger, bitterness, depression, emotional problems, fights and violence.

Allah brought the Islamic religion to His people so that they can live in peace at all times. The religion of Muslims was first taught by the Prophet Mohammad in the 7th Century A. D. The Muslims worship one God, Allah, and consider Mohammad as the last prophet. Excerpts from the Holy Qur'an say, "Divine Guidance; the Creator, the Master, and the Sovereign, created man, and bestowed upon him the faculties of speaking, learning, understanding and the ability to discern right from wrong–good from Evil. He granted him specific freedoms of choice, of will and of action. He gave him authority to acquire and make use of his surroundings."

Essentially, Allah gave the mankind autonomy, appointing him as His vicegerent on the Earth. When the Lord of the universe appointed man as his vicegerent, He warned him very clearly and precisely, leaving no doubt as to account of such a different of opinion. They may put forward their own arguments in support of their opinions, and leave the decision to the highest court if it is some judicial matter or to the legislative body of the community if it concerns them. Then either one or both of the divergent opinions will prevail. But it should be noted particularly that no difference can be allowed in the basic principles of Islam, nor in such matters as may lead to the formation of a new community. It is the duty of every Muslim, men, woman, and children, to read the Qur'an and understand it according to his own capacity. If any one of us attains some knowledge of understanding of it by study, contemplation, and the test of life, both outward and inward, it is his duty, according to his capacity, to instruct others, and share with them they joy and peace, which result from contact with the spiritual world."

The Islamic prayer for world peace is, "In the name of Allah, the beneficent, the merciful: Praise be to the Lord of the

Three Solutions for World Peace

Universe who has created us and made us into tribes and nations that we may know each other, not that we may despise each other. If the enemy inclines towards peace, do thou also incline towards peace, and trust in God. For the Lord is one that hears and knows all things. And the servants of God most gracious are those who walk on the earth in humility, and when we address them, we say, "Peace."

(SURAH): In the Surah, which teaches about prayer it says, "For if we can pray aright, it means that we have some knowledge of Allah and His attributes, of His relation to us and His creation, which includes ourselves; that we glimpse the source from which we come, and that final goal which is our spiritual destiny under Allah's true judgment; then we offer ourselves to Allah and seek His light. Prayer is the heart of religion and faith. We think in devotion of Allah's name and His nature; we praise Him for His creation and His cherishing care; we call to mind the realities, seen and unseen; we offer Him worship and ask for His guidance; and we know the straight from the crooked path by the light of His grace that illuminates the righteous".

Al-Fatha (Suratul-Fatiha Surah AlFatihah, Al Fatiha) prayer begins by saying, "In the name of Allah, most Gracious, most Merciful. Praise be to Allah, the cherisher and sustainer of the world. Most gracious, most merciful, Master of the Day of

Judgment, you alone do we worship, and your aid we seek, show us the straightway. The way of those whom you has bestowed your Grace, those whose is not wrath, and who go not astray."

The Muslim prayer for world peace is, (in Arabic) "Rabbanaa atinaa fid – dunyea hasa natanw-wa fil aak hirati hasanotanuw-wa ginaa 'azaaban-naar (Holy Qur'an 002:201) bi rahmatika ya Ar-hamr-Rahimeen." (In English) "Our Lord gives us good in this world and good in the hereafter, and defends us from the torment of the (hell) fire with thy kindness, O Benevolent of the benevolent." (Contributed by Al-waamirali) "Allahumma ya mowlana antas – salaamu wa minkast – salaam, wailaika yar jaus-salaam, haiyyina rabbana bis-salaam, wa adkhillnadaras-Salaam, tabarakta rasbana wa-talaita, ya Zal Jalall wal Ikran." (In English) O' God O' our Master you are eternal life and everlasting peace by your essence and attributes. The everlasting peace is from you and it returns to you. O' our sustainer grants us the life of true peace and usher us into the abode of peace. O' Glorious and Bounteous one. You are blessed and sublime. (Contributed by professor Nooracellah Juma University of Alberta and Prof. Abdul S. Hencam) Muslim prayers in the Holy Qur'an offer many prayers of peace and the divine name has power, blessings and spiritual help for all the Muslim believers. Some of the names in the Holy Qur'an are, "Ya Haakim, Ya Wakil, Ya Fattah, Ya Salaam." Such names as, "Huwal Laahul, Khaaliqul Baari'ul Musawwiru Lahul," which means, "He is Allah, the creator, the shaper out of naught, the Fashioner?" "Yusabbihu lahun maa fis-samaawaati Wal-arz: wa huwal- AZiizul-Hakim," (Q: 59:24), means, "His is the Most beautiful of names. All that is in the heavens and in the Earth glorifieth Him, and He is the mighty, the Wise."

DEFINITIONS

(1) Ya-HaaKim – the Wise: He who has wisdom in all orders and actions (2) Ya-Wakill – The Trustee: He who provides a solution for every problem in the best manner. (3) Ya-Fattah – the decider: He who opens the solution to all problems and eliminates obstacles. (4) Ya- Salaam – the Source of Peace: He who frees His Servants from all danger and obstruction.

The Holy Qur'an teaches that the way to overcome difficulties is through abundant prayers and divine remembrance, which creates courage, strength, inspiration and pure intention in one's being. It teaches that God has given divine remembrance and divine light to human minds for the deaf, the blind and for those who are the enemies of God to come to the knowledge of obedience and submit to Allah's Orders. (Holy Qur'an 2:255)

I continue to compare and review Muslim prayers. They are the same as the Christian prayers. I found the name of Allah in prayers to be very fascinating and inspirational with divine attributes and divine power. Ya Qudir, Ya Nasi, Ya Tauba, Ya Salaam all mean the following: O' powerful, O' Helper, O' Forgiver, O' the Source of Peace. The Holy Qur'an teaches Muslim believers to continually seek forgiveness of sins and mercy of Allah. It teaches that Muslim believers must understand the nature of sins, including inward and outward sins. They should strive to remain pure and humble.

When I read the Qur'an to this point, I picked up my pen, as I was shocked. I began to write because I want someone to hear me and readers to read my writing and understand that most of the world violence, war and killing every minute comes from the Muslim world. Beginning from Medina, Mecca and has spread all over the world and continues up until today. The Muslim world and their religion are two different entities, two different people. I will say that fifty percent of Muslims have never followed the teaching of the Qur'an and five percent of the Muslim world followed the teaching of the Qur'an, while ninety-five percent have never, or will never follow the teaching of Qur'an.

Persecution of other religions occurred with brutal killings and war against other Muslim nations has occurred. Now we have war within the Muslim nation where a dictator is ordering the army to mass murder the people they supposedly protect. They did not follow what Allah said in the Holy Qur'an up to the point that they entered the Mosque Holy Worship place to kill their own people on Friday, the Holy day of Worship. They killed so many protesters during the Ramadan worship celebration.

The Muslim religion and people are not practicing what they are teaching and preaching. They are not following the Holy Book of Qur'an. I realized that if Muslims, Christians and Jews pray the same; why are they constantly persecuting Christians? Why are husbands killing the wife and/or children for reading the Bible? Islam is supposed to be a religion of peace, but the people have turned it around and hid underneath the name to do evil and to do whatever pleases them.

Some do not follow the instruction and the Islam teaching, as it is written in the Holy Qur'an. It was sent by Allah for world peace, but they never use it for peace; they turn it around and do the opposite, using it for war and violence.

This action from some of the Muslims has reduced the power and devalued the meaning of the Islam religion all over the world.

Even though they have more resources and money than some other nations in the world because of rich soil flowing with oil, a great blessing from Allah, (OLD TESTAMENT PROMISE

TO HAGER); they are still not in peace. They are not pleased with their land, the way of peace they do not seek, and pursue.

Furthermore, I don't know when they will come to the knowledge of peace in the world. Therefore, they are not doing anything to solve or help in terms of solving the world peace.

The Muslim world is not in any way contributing to the world peace. In this powerful prayer for world peace, there is no mention of peace. They call on the name of Allah with attributes of beneficent, merciful, with praises of creator of all tribes and nations, most importantly the prayer wants us to trust God. The prayer mentioned a peace acknowledgement that God knows all things and is gracious.

The Islamic prayer for world peace does not mention the solution for world peace. What are we people in the entire world need to do to achieve and have peace in the world? I would like to pause and give the summary of the beginning of the history of the descendants of Abraham that also led to the three great religions in the world.

Three Solutions for World Peace

Chapter Thirteen

History of Ishmael and Isaac

The Holy Bible Scripture speaks of Abram's wife Sarai. Sarai had a maid and her name was called Hager. She was an Egyptian woman. "Now Sarai Abram's wife bore him no children; and she had a handmaid, an Egyptian, whose name was Hagar. And Sa'rai said to A'bram, 'Behold now, the Lord has restrained me from bearing: I pray you, go in to my maid; it may be that I may obtain children by her.' And A'bram hearkened to the voice of Sa'rai. And, Sa'rai A'bram's, wife took Hagar, her maid the Egyptian, after A'bram had dwelt ten years in the land of Canaan, and gave her to her husband Abram to be his wife. And he went into Hagar, and she conceived and when she saw that she had conceived her mistress was despised in her eye." (Gen. 16:1-5)

Three Solutions for World Peace

Hagar bears the child and his name was called Ishmael. "And the Lord visited Sarah as He had said, and the Lord did to Sarah as he had spoken. Sarah conceived, and bore Abraham a son in his old age, at the set time of which God had spoken to him. And Abraham called the name of Sarah's bore to him, Isaac. Abraham was 100 years old when Isaac was born to him. And the child grew up and was weaned: And Abraham made a great feast the same day that Isaac was weaned. And Sarah saw the son of Hager the Egyptian which she had born to Abraham, mocking." (Gen 21:1-3, 5)

Both two boys lived in the tent with their parents. Ishmael did not like his little brother Isaac; they did not get along very well together and this made Sarai very uncomfortable, as well as angry. It came to pass one day that Sarai told Abrahm that Ishmael did not like Isaac; he did not treat him kindly and this made her angry. She said she did not want the two boys to grow up together in the same tent. Sarai told Abraham to send the maid and her child away. Abrahm was not happy about the decision or the solution from his wife. That night Abraham had a vision. The Lord spoke to him, "Do not be afraid or troubled about Ishmael and Hager. I the Lord will take care of Ishmael, and will make him a great nation, because he was his seed." (Gen. 21:13)

"God heard the voice of the lad, and the angel of God called to Hagar out of heaven, and said to her, "What ails you, Hager?" Fear not; for God has heard the voice of the lad where he is. Arise, lift up the lad, and hold him in your hand, for I will make him a great nation. God opened her eyes, and she saw a well of water; and she went, and filled the bottle with water and gave the lad to drink." (Gen. 21:17-19).

God heard the cry of Hager and her son; God told Hagar that He would take care of the boy and make the boy a great nation on Earth. Abraham offered Isaac his only son and the Lord spoke to him and said, "By myself have I sworn, says the Lord, for because you have done this thing, and have not withheld your son, your only son; that in blessing I will bless you and in multiplying I will multiply your seed as the stars of the heaven, and as the sand which is upon the sea shore; and your seed shall possess the gate of his enemies; And in your seed shall all the nations of earth be blessed because you have obeyed my voice." (Gen 22:16-18)

The Lord God Almighty fulfills and continues to fulfill His promise from Old Testament to New Testament. All Christians are all the children of Abraham. Abraham died at age of 175 years old. Ishmael grew up in the desert; he became a wild man and so did his children. Ishmael came to be the father of many people and his descendants are many. Ishmael continued to contact his father,

Abraham. Ishmael was 90-years old when his father Abraham died. Because of the burial of their father, the two boys, now men, met each other after they had been separated for many years. They both gathered together with the members of their household to pay the last respects to their father Abraham. "And his sons Isaac and Ishmael buried their father in the cave of Machpelah, in the field of Ephron the son of Zohar the Hittite, which is before Mamre." (Gen. 25:9)

What a reunion would that be on that day. The two brothers separated when they were young, see each other at adulthood. Ishmael settled in the land of Puran, between Canaan and the mountain of Sinai- God was with him. "Now these are the generations of Ishmael, Abraham's son whom Hagar the Egyptian, Sarah's handmade, bore to Abraham and these are the names of the sons of Ishmael. By their names, according to their generations: The first born of Ishmael, nabajoth, and Kedar, and Adbeel, and Mibsams, and Mishima, and Dumah, and Massa, Hadas, and Tema, Je'tur Naphish, and kedemah; these are the sons of Ishmael and these are their names, by towns, and by their Castles: Twelve Princes according to their nations. Ishmael died at the age of 137 years old. The twelve sons became the founders of many Arab tribes or colonies the Ishmaelites spread over desert spaces of Northern Arabia from the Red Sea to the Euphrates. (Gen. 37:25-

28, 39:1) God fulfilled His promise to the Ishmaelites as He said. They became great nations and wealthy nations where oil is flowing in their land like a river.

The Book of Genesis is where we read about Adam and Eve as well. We also read about the first worldwide flood and where God changed the language of people, scattering them, which was called the Babel era. We learn about the Israelite's nation beginning with Abraham and God's two great promises to Abram. First that he will make him a great nation and His seed like sea sands in the shore. Hagar is the mother of Abraham's first son, Ishmael mentioned in the Qur'an. Hagar's son, Ishmael means, "God hears." Abraham was 86 years when Ishmael was born. Hagar abandoned her camp, but God came to her aid. (Gen. 16:20) And as for Ishmael, I have heard you: "I will surely bless him; I will make Him fruitful and I will greatly increase his numbers. He will be the father of twelve rulers, and I will make him into a great nation. My Question is: Why are these two brothers who are descendants of Abraham fighting up until today with all the blessings of God given to them, which is more than the blessings of other nations on Earth?

I continue to research the solution for world peace and I decided to look into the Christian religion.

Three Solutions for World Peace

Chapter Fourteen

The Roman Empire Period from 63 B.C.

The Roman Empire period began in 63 B.C.: In the year 63 B.C. Pompey, the Roman general, captured Jerusalem and the provinces of Palestine, which became subject to Rome. The local government was entrusted part of the time to princes and the rest of the time to procurators who were appointed by the Emperors.

Herod the Great was ruler of all of Palestine at the time of Christ's birth. The Prophet Isaiah in the Old Testament in Isaiah 7:14 and in the Gospel of Matthew and Luke in the New Testament revealed the virginity of the mother of Jesus. The Biblical revelation of Jesus' virgin conception and birth is commonly opposed by liberal scholars and some cults. The revelation from the Books of Matthew and Luke are very clear. The importance of the virgin birth cannot be overemphasized. In order for our redeemer to qualify to pay for our sins and bring salvation he must be in one person, fully human, sinless and fully divine. The virgin birth satisfies all three of these requirements: (1) The only way Jesus could be born a human being was to be born of a woman, (2) The only way he could be sinless was to be conceived by the Holy Spirit, (3) The only way he could be divine was to have God as his Father. As a result, his conception was not by natural, but by supernatural means; "… the Holy one to be born will be called the Son of God." (Lk. 1:35) Jesus Christ is therefore revealed to us as one divine person with two natures divine and sinless human.

The Gospel of Matthew opens with the genealogy, which traces Jesus' ancestral lineage through the paternal line of Joseph, even though Joseph was not Jesus' biological father he was his legal father. God promised that the Messiah would be a descendant of Abraham. (Gen.12:3; 22:18) The word "Christ" means "Anointed", "Messiah." (Dan. 9:25-26) Jesus was anointed with the Holy Spirit. He was anointed as a prophet as well to bring knowledge and truth. (Deut.18:15) He was anointed as a Priest to offer the sacrifice and cancel the guilt and sins. (Ps. 110:4; Heb. 10:10-14) He was anointed as King to rule, guide and establish the kingdom of righteousness. (Zec. 9:9) According to the record of genealogy of Jesus Christ, he is the son of David, the son of

Abraham. Jesus began His teaching at the age of thirty years old, after John the Baptist baptized him.

The Gospel of Matthew presents Jesus as the fulfillment of Israel's prophetic hope. Jesus fulfills Old Testament prophecy in his birth, birthplace, taken to Egypt and returned from Egypt, lived in Nazareth, His teaching and his healing ministry, His role as God's servant, the teaching of parables, His triumphal entry into Jerusalem, His arrest by the Roman Solders, His death, burial and His resurrection.

We are waiting for His return to Judge the dead and the living. All the eyes shall see Him. Christianity is based on the believer's relationship with the Lord and Savior of all people of the world.

Three Solutions for World Peace

Chapter Fifteen

Christian Religion Prayer for World Peace

The Christian Prayer for world peace is, "He shall judge between nations, and shall decide for many people and they shall beat their swords into plow shares and their spears into pruning hooks; nation shall not lift up sword against nations, neither shall they learn war any more." Jesus Christ's teachings during His earthly ministry were as follows, "Blessed are the peace- makers for they shall be called the children of God." (Mt.5:9) "But I say to you that hear, love your enemies; do good to those who hate you: Bless those who curse you; pray for those who abuse you. To those who strike you on the check offer the other also; and from those who take away your cloak, do not with hold your coat as well. Give to everyone who begs from you, and those who take away your goods, do not ask them again. And as you wish that others would do to you, do so to them." These Bible quotes are from the Sermon on the Mount also known as Christ's Sermon on the Mount.

It says blessed are the peacemakers for they shall be called the children of God. Peacemakers are those who have been reconciled to God and the Lord Jesus Christ. They have peace with Christ through the Cross. They are now working hard to bring others to Christ through witnesses around the world to the sinners and the lost. They also work hard to bring their enemies to have peace with God through the forgiven power of Jesus Christ. God's blessings on the lives of His people are very essential. God wants us to do well to those who do bad to us to return love for hatred. This Bible verse is teaching us how to live a peaceable life with others. This teaching opens the door of how to work towards world peace and prepares us for the road to world peace.

Christ begins His sermon with blessings for He came into the world to bless us. He bestowed the blessings as one having authority, or as one that can command the blessing, from here on Earth to eternity. The Old Testament ended with a curse. (Mal. 4:6) The gospel of God in New Testament begins with blessings. Each of the blessings Christ here pronounces has a double intention: The peacemakers are happy, the wisdom that is from above is first pure, and then peaceable; the blessed ones are pure towards God, and peaceable towards men. The peacemakers are those who have a peaceable disposition. It is to love and desire, to delight in peace.

Loving your enemy could lead to world peace, but it has a long way to go in order to be achieved. Jesus said, "Where to then shall liken the men of this generation? And to what are they like? They are like children sitting in the marketplace, and calling one to another, and saying, we have piped to you, and you have not dances, we have mourned to you, and you have not wept." (Lk.7:31-32)

I will move forward to review the violence in the World War II.

Three Solutions for World Peace

Chapter Sixteen

World War II and It's Violence

World War II, in which my father, Thomas Abifasere Oyetuga Balogun, was one of the men drafted by the British Government. At that time, the nation of Nigeria was under the British colony, thus the reason for the drafting of my father. My father, according to him, was drafted on his job where he worked as a machine cleaner/operator at the Lagos Daily Newspaper.

He went to war from Lagos Nigeria in 1939 and came back to Lagos in December of 1945. In the beginning, he had a traditional wedding with my mother, then they both came back to Lagos that weekend. Monday he went to work and was drafted. He just came back home to say goodbye to my mother because he was ordered to stay in the army camp for training. He told my

Three Solutions for World Peace

mother that he would be going to war in Germany. My mother waited for him until he returned back to Nigeria in 1945. One person caused World War II, which spread to all the nations. Millions of Jewish people, Africans and people from all other nations perished. The wounds of the war have never healed to some people in all the nations until today.

I remember that my Dad always tell us the story of his American friend who died in his arms. The man prayed for him before he closed his eyes. The man prayed and asked God to please return my Dad back to his newlywed wife that was waiting for him in Lagos. God answered my Dad's friend's prayer when the war ended in 1945 and my Dad returned back to Africa in Lagos, Nigeria in December of 1945. He was born in 1914 and later died in the year 1978.

Is there any peace in the world since 1945? The answer is No. The United Nations General Assembly has been looking for a way or the best way to put stop the violence in the Middle East and North Africa, West Africa and to other parts of the nations in the world since the end of Second World War, but it is impossible for them. Violence in other parts of the world such as East, West, South Africa, South Asia and the entire nations of Earth has been happening ever since.

Three Solutions for World Peace

The ending of World War II supposedly provided a new beginning of world peace and provided a dynamic basis for evaluation of the quality of world peace that covers all countries in the world. The end of World War II supposedly provided systematic foundations for peace within the global system. According to my observation, the UN System has never been effective in providing peace and security for the people in all the nations of Earth. War and violence are increasing continuously in a dramatic way every day.

We have to look back to what has been happening since 1945 after the Second World War and the establishment of the United Nations. Beginning from 1946 to 2011, right after the Second World War in 1946 on July 22th, 1946, there was a bombing of The King David Hotel, at the British military head quarter in Jerusalem by which resulted in 91 military and civilian deaths. In 1947, 19th of July, there was a terrorist attack on four locations in Haifa, killing a British constable and as many as 12 people were injured. In the same year, on December 30th, Irgun threw several grenades at a group of workers outside of the Haifa Oil Refinery, which resulted in the death of six people and 42 people were injured. The attack was escalated on the Jewish refinery workers by Arab refinery workers resulting in 39 deaths and 49 people injured. In 1949 on the 5th of August, 12 People were killed and dozens injured in the Menarsha Synagogue attack in Damascus. In 1956, on the 16th of June, a bomb explosion in Nicosia left one dead and six people injured. In 1958, on the 15th of August, 3 people died in a bomb blast in Beirut and as many as ten people were injured. In 1965, on June 26th, two explosions took place near a restaurant. In the 1965 Saigon bombing during the Vietnam War 42 people were killed and more than 80 people were injured. In 1967 on November 12th, a bomb explosion on board of British European Airways flight 284 near Rhodes, killed all 66 people on board. In 1969, the 12th of December, the Piazza Fontana bombing in Milano occurred-17 people died and 88 people were injured. On Feb 3rd, 1987, Islamic Fundamentalists, who are conservative religious Islamists, seek to return to Islamic value and Islamic law such as Sharia law. In 1992, on June 29th, the Head of State of Algeria was shot at Annaba. In 1993, former Prime Minister of Algeria Kasdi Merbah, was killed by gunmen.

The United Nations, an organization, which consists of 191 countries, continues to strive to attain international peace and security since its establishment on June 25th, 1945; all the delegates are from all the nations. The General Assembly, the Security Council, the Economic and Social Council, the Secretariat and International Court of Justice work together to achieve world peace to no avail. The Security Council with all its responsibility for maintaining peace and security between the nations in time of war and violence is not working properly as it should be working. The Security Council's objective which is to look for peace of all nations and settle all the differences conflicts between the two or three nations is not working. Since 1948 more than 750,000 people have served in many nations in order to keep peace. More than 1800 peacekeepers have lost their lives. In 2003, 37,000 personnel including troops, civilian police and military serve from 89 countries.

UN peacekeepers always intervene in other situations to break the violence or conflicts. A ceasefire is issued if the war is already ongoing. They may even impose economic sanctions or military actions. Sometimes, the UN peacekeeping fails on its obligation. For example, during the 1990's, UN had troops operating during the civil war in Somalia. In 1995 the UN's operations were cancelled or ended in Somalia without fulfilling its mission. This means that they failed in their support in regards to the Somalian people and nation. In 1994, 35,000 troops were sent during the attacks in Bosnia and Herzegovina. UN intervention and operations in Kashmir and between the nations from 1998 to the year 2000 with Kashmir, Cyprus, Lebanon, Suez, Cambodia, and Mozambique, Congo Central African Republic, East Timor,

Kosovo, Sierra Leone, Ethiopia, Salvador, Nicaragua, Haiti and South Africa.

UN operations are in Iraq and Libya since the violence broke out. Billions of dollars have been spent on war and violence all over the nations in the world. Thousands of people have died. Billions of properties and houses were destroyed. Millions of pounds of food have been wasted while many people in the other parts of the world have no food to eat. The more the UN tried to keep peace in the world, the more war and violence emerged and continues to this day.

Another example is the conflict between the Sunnis and Shiites. On October 27th, 2009, an extremist group claimed responsibility for the Baghdad bombing the Islamic state of Iraq; a Sunni extremist group, that includes Al Qaeda, claimed responsibility for the bombing that killed 160 Iraqis. (Washington Post 10/27/09) In November 2010, a Baghdad church was held hostage and 52 people were killed as the security forces entered the Catholic Church to free the hostages. (NY Times Terrorist)

Attacks continue by groups of the people in the name of their religions (the Taliban and Al-Qaeda). Why can't they just come forward and tell the world what they need so that they can stop the killing of innocent people around the world?

For example, on September 11, 2001 in the United States, thousands of innocent people lost their lives. On October 25th, 2009, a deadly bombing occurred that was the worst in Iraq attack in two years-132 people were killed and more than 500 people were wounded (CNN 10/25/09). All these episodes in all the nations were caused by political violence and religious violence, tribal war, land claiming war and violence where one country claims the land of another country. The beginning and ending of most land claiming violence and political violence from a dictator are very difficult to determine when it is going to end.

In regards the September 11, 2001 Islamic terrorist attack on the United States, Islamic terrorists hijacked private airlines that were headed to symbolic targets in New York and Washington DC. There have been Taliban operations in Afghanistan in late 2001 as well. Terrorism continues to emerge, the continuing effect of terrorism damage and the impact against all nations is very hard to know at this point because we do not know when they are going to stop. Ten thousand and more protesters in the streets all across Syria are campaigning against the dictator leader and his regime. The violence and killing goes on every day, including Fridays, which is the Muslim's Holy worship day.

Uprisings continue as well in Libya against the dictator leader where violence continues and many lives are cut short, including the innocent lives of children. Shortages of food, medical supplies and shelters are common among these nations as well. The suffering is great upon many.

Upon reviewing all these violent wars and killings in the world, it comes to me clearly that people of the world are missing one important point that holds the lives and liberty together. Without these three words that must start right from day when an individual is born, that is automatically transferred from the parents to the newborn child, which will grow with the child everyday until he or she becomes an adult and uses it, practices it and manifests it to other people around them.

Chapter Seventeen

United Nations Establishment and Operations

The United Nations existence, since it started in 1945, which continues up until today does not achieve world peace at any given year as it was anticipated when it was founded. Instead it creates more violence, the presidents of the member nations do not follow rules, they don't want to be corrected as to what they are doing to their own people. For example, what is going on in Libya and Syria etc., including the other nations around them. They have no respect for any human rights organization; they have no concerns whatsoever for human life of their own citizens and they have no respect in following other's human rights organizations recommendations. They continuously mass-murder their own people; many children are dying from lack of food, shelter and medical assistants.

Three Solutions for World Peace

All these presidents are also followers of certain religious beliefs. What is surprising is that they will show up at the United Nations Summit as if they have done some good. I have concluded that nothing has been solved or any solutions reached at the UN Summit in regards to world peace. The UN Summit was supposed to be where all the nations sit together to solve the nation's problems together. It is supposed to be where all the presidents of the nation's rejoice and create peace within the neighboring countries, plan how peace on Earth can be achieved and delegate how nations will decide to stop waging war on each other.

The Summit is where every nation will discusses how to assist other nations that have no food to include how to solve tribal problems with other nations or within the nations. The Summit is where they can talk to each other about humanitarian services around the world by taking the people of their nation to voluntarily help other people that are suffering in other nations.

At the UN Summit conference the presidents' shake hands, but they never shake their mind off from war against each other. Some of presidents in the world are hypocrites, selfish, self-centered, self-righteous and full of abusive of power that the people that voted for them gave them. They are not representing the people; they are representing themselves and doing their own thing, may God forgive them.

Therefore, upon reviewing the United Nations operations, which is supposed to bring peace to the world if all the presidents of all the nations follow the UN directions, decisions and procedures, the world would have been in harmony. The money spent on war would have helped to reduce the hunger and thirst and lack of electricity in other parts of the world where children are dying everyday because there is no rain for crops, no food and no water to drink. I concluded that United Nations cannot bring people peace or stop the violence in the world. I found out that one important thing that is missing makes it difficult for the UN to achieve the goal of peace in the world. My search for the solution to world peace cannot be found through the United Nations and I continue my search.

Three Solutions for World Peace

Chapter Eighteen

Suggestion & Advice to the Super Power Nation Leaders & United Nations

In the Month of May 2012, the world leaders met to discuss the problems of Afghanistan, one of the Arab countries, after they have been there for many years in order to keep peace in that nation. Many soldiers have lost their lives in all the NATO countries to no avail because the problems continue. Some of the NATO nations have cut their deals with Afghanistan. My Questions is: Why is it that these countries face and continue to help those who are not in need of help? Instead of helping the people of African continents where millions of children and adults are dying everyday for lack of water, energy, food and all other things that can make people live a normal life.

Three Solutions for World Peace

NATO countries consistent of over fifty nations; they were trying to make peace in one nation, while their own soldiers were perishing everyday. Thousands of children have no father, and thousands of women have no husband. They cause destruction upon the lives of their own citizens when they should have sent those soldiers to all the fifty-seven African countries to help, educate, provide a permanent solution for water, energy and food. In this way they will make more friends, at the same time they will not lose any of their soldiers.

This action will create more peace in the world where the Arab countries will see and be jealous. Instead of fighting and killing their own people, they will copy the way of peace. For example, how many years have US soldiers stayed in Iraq and worked with the Iraq? These are soldiers for peace. How many soldiers lost their lives in Iraq, after they decided to leave? Up until today the Iraqi people are still killing each other through the suicide bombers everyday.

If all the NATO countries spent five years to concentrate on the African continent, offering help to stabilize the lives of people and children in all the fifty-seven countries in the continent, it will be a good example for other countries to follow. I believe that this will help them to think twice before they keep killing their own brothers and sisters, including, killing their own children.

We have to expect this action from any country where there is a dictator leadership. One person does not care if everybody in his country is dying, if so far his own family is under protection. Human beings are born to be selfish and heartless, unless God is in the heart of that leader. We have to remember Sadam Hussein in Iraq and Moamar Khadafy in Libya. He wasted the lives of his own people until he was captured.

I strictly advise NATO to leave countries of violence for at least five years. The leaders should try to diversify their humanitarian services to clean water, nutritional food for children and health care services for all the people in under-developed countries.

Three Solutions for World Peace

Three Solutions for World Peace

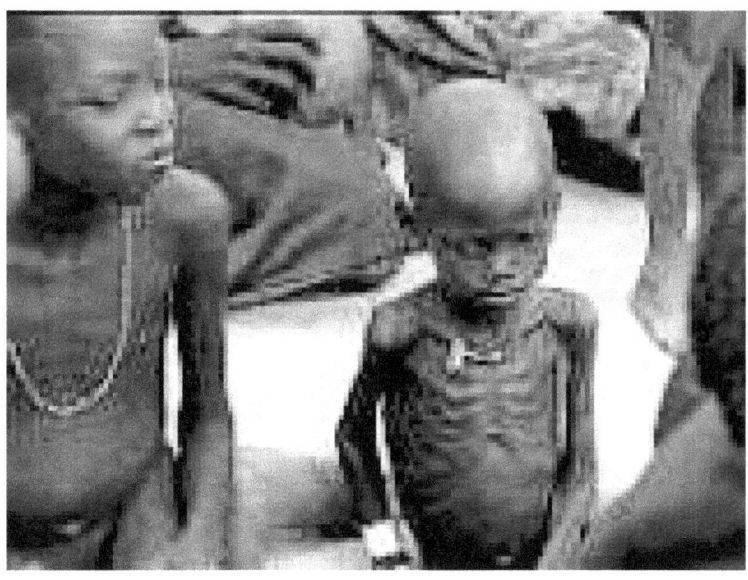

Three Solutions for World Peace

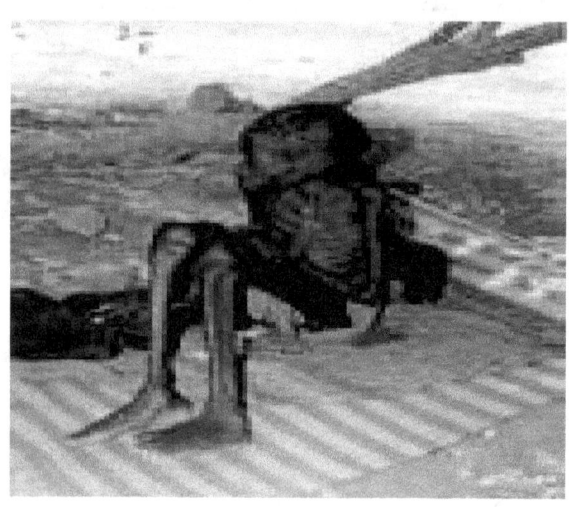

Three Solutions for World Peace

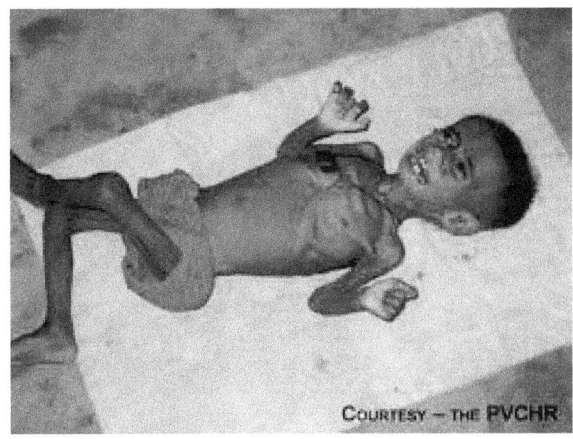

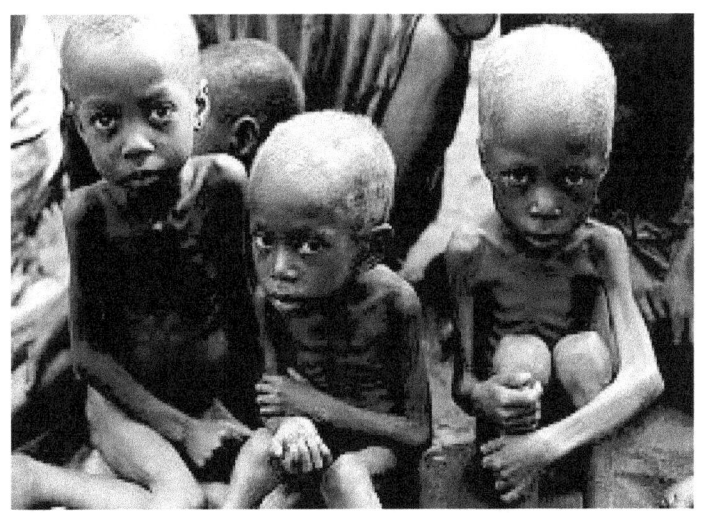

Three Solutions for World Peace

Three Solutions for World Peace

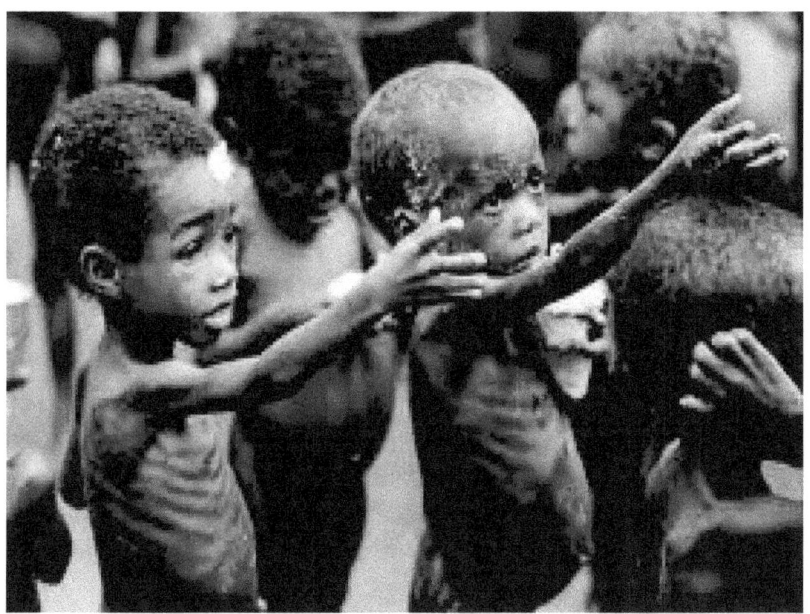

Three Solutions for World Peace

Chapter Nineteen

Food Program Organization FAO & WFP - Reports

THESE ARE FOOD PROGRAM ORGANIZATIONS FAO & WFP - UNITED NATIONS' REPORTS:

14 September 2010, Rome - FAO and the United Nations World Food Program (WFP) today said that the number of hungry people in the world remains unacceptably high despite expected recent gains that have pushed the figure below 1 billion.

The new estimate of the number of people who will suffer chronic hunger this year is 925 million — 98 million down from 1.023 billion in 2009.

"But with a child dying every six seconds because of undernourishment related problems, hunger remains the world's largest tragedy and scandal," said FAO Director-General Jacques Diouf. "This is absolutely unacceptable."

MDGs Achievement Difficult

The continuing high global hunger level, ". . . makes it extremely difficult to achieve not only the first Millennium Development Goal (MDG), but also the rest of the MDGs," Diouf warned.

"The achievement of the international hunger reduction target is at serious risk," he added, further noting that recent increases in food prices, if they persist, could hamper efforts to further reduce the numbers of the world's hungry."

"Vigorous and urgent action by nations and the world has been effective in helping to halt galloping hunger numbers," said WFP Executive Director, Josette Sheeran. "But this is no time to relax. We must keep hunger on the run to ensure stability and to protect lives and dignity."

Flagship Report

The new hunger figure is contained in the annual flagship report, "The State of Food Insecurity in the world" (SOFI) to be jointly published by FAO and WFP in October. The figure was released in advance of the September 20-22 Summit meeting in New York called to speed progress towards achievement of the United

Nations Millennium Development Goals (MDGs), the first of which is to end poverty and hunger.

Last May Diouf also launched a **"1 billion hungry campaign"** aimed at inciting world leaders into taking firm and urgent action to end hunger. More than half a million people have already signed an online petition calling on politicians to make hunger reduction their top priority and a million are expected by the end of this year.

Yukiko Omura, Vice President of IFAD, said, "The world's hungry are not just numbers. They are people - poor women and men struggling to bring up their children and give them a better life; and they are youth trying to build a future for them. It is ironic that the majority of them actually live in rural areas of developing countries. Indeed, over 70 percent of the world's extremely poor- those people, who live on less than $1.25 a day, live in rural areas. That's a billion people, and four out of five of them are farmers to some extent or the other."

Economic Growth, Lower Prices

The 2010 lower global hunger number resulted largely from renewed economic growth expected this year-particularly in developing countries-and the drop in food prices since mid-2008. The recent increase in food prices, if it continues, will create obstacles in the further reduction of hunger.

Of the eight Millennium Development Goals solemnly agreed by the UN in 2000, MDG 1 pledged to halve the proportion of hungry people from 20 to 10 percent by 2015. With five years to go, that proportion currently stands at 16 percent, however.

Previously, in 1996, a World Food Summit had for the first time set a quantitative target of halving the number of hungry people from roughly 800 million in 1990-92 to about 400 million by 2015. Achieving that goal would mean cutting the number of hungry by over 500 million in the next five years.

Structural Problem

The fact that historically the number of undernourished continued to increase even in periods of high growth and relatively low prices indicate that hunger is a structural problem, FAO said. It is therefore clear that economic growth, while essential, will not be sufficient to eliminate hunger within an acceptable period of time, FAO added. But, "Success stories do exist in Africa, in Asia and in Latin America," Diouf noted. These experiences need to be scaled up and replicated. Globally, the 2010 hunger figure marked a decline of 9.6 percent from the 2009 level. This reduction was mostly concentrated in Asia, where 80 million fewer people were estimated to be going hungry this year. In sub-Saharan Africa the drop was much smaller-about 12 million-and one out of three people there would continue to be undernourished.

Key Findings

Other key findings of the report included:

• Two thirds of the world's undernourished live in just seven countries — Bangladesh, China, the Democratic Republic of Congo, Ethiopia, India, Indonesia and Pakistan.

• The region with the most undernourished people continues to be Asia and the Pacific with 578 million.

• The proportion of undernourished people remains highest in sub-Saharan Africa at 30 percent in 2010, or 239 million.

• Progress varies widely at country level. As of 2005-2007 (the most recent period for which complete data was available), the Congo, Ghana, Mali and Nigeria had already achieved MDG1 in sub-Saharan Africa, and Ethiopia and others are close to achieving it. However, the proportion of undernourished rose to 69 percent in the Democratic Republic of Congo.

• In Asia, Armenia, Myanmar and Vietnam had already achieved MDG1 and China is close to doing so.

- In Latin America and the Caribbean, Guyana, Jamaica and Nicaragua had already achieved MDG1 while Brazil is coming close.

2012 World Hunger and Poverty Facts and Statistics

World Hunger Education Service

(Also see **World Child Hunger Facts**)

This fact sheet is divided into the following sections:

- **Hunger concepts and definitions**
- **Number of hungry people in the world**
- **Does the world produce enough food to feed everyone?**
- **Causes of hunger**
- **Progress in reducing the number of hungry people**
- **Micronutrients**

Hunger Concepts and Definitions:

Hunger is a term, which has three meanings (Oxford English Dictionary 1971)

- The uneasy or painful sensation caused by want of food; craving appetite. Also the exhausted condition caused by want of food;
- the want or scarcity of food in a country;
- a strong desire or craving.

World hunger refers to the second definition, aggregated to the world level. The related technical term (in this case operationalized in medicine) is malnutrition.[1]

Malnutrition is a general term that indicates a lack of some or all-nutritional elements necessary for human health (Medline Plus Medical Encyclopedia).

There are two basic types of malnutrition. The first and most important is protein-energy malnutrition--the lack of enough protein (from meat and other sources) and food that provides energy (measured in calories) which all of the basic food groups provide. This is the type of malnutrition that is referred to when world hunger is discussed. The second type of malnutrition, also very important, is micronutrient (vitamin and mineral) deficiency.

This is not the type of malnutrition that is referred to when world hunger is discussed, though it is certainly very important.

Recently there has also been a move to include obesity as a third form of malnutrition. Considering obesity as malnutrition expands the previous usual meaning of the term, which referred to poor nutrition due to lack of food inputs.[2] It is poor nutrition, but it is certainly not typically due to a lack of calories, but rather too many (although poor food choices, often due to poverty, are part of the problem). Obesity will not be considered here, although obesity is certainly a health problem and is increasingly considered as a type of malnutrition.]

Protein-energy malnutrition (PEM) is the most lethal form of malnutrition/hunger. It is basically a lack of calories and protein. Humans convert food into energy, and the energy contained in food is measured by calories. Protein is necessary for key body functions including provision of essential amino acids and development and maintenance of muscles.

Number of Hungry People in the World

925 million hungry people in 2010

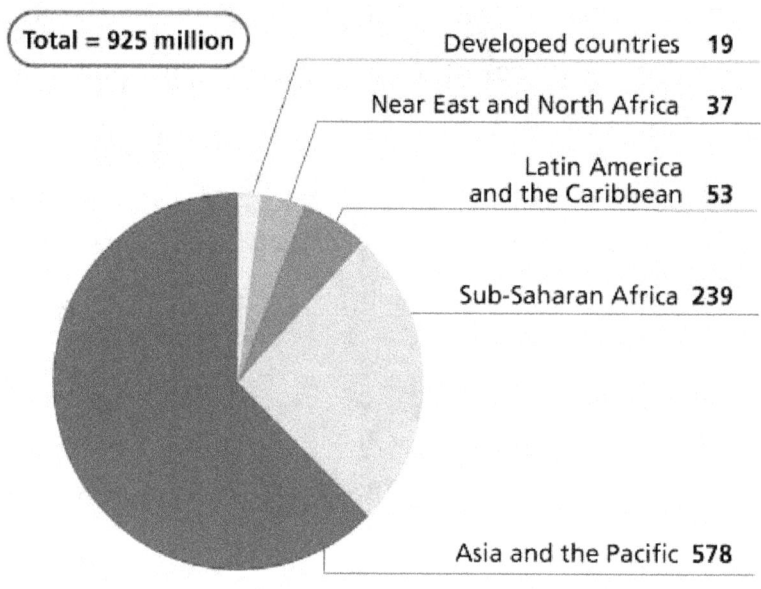

Source: FAO.

No one really knows how many people are malnourished. The statistic most frequently cited is that of the United Nations Food and Agriculture Organization, which measures 'under-nutrition'. The FAO did not publish an estimate in its most recent publication, "The State of Food Insecurity in the World 2011" as it is undertaking a major revision of how it estimates food insecurity. (FAO 2011 p. 10) The 2010 estimate, the most recent, says that 925 million people were undernourished in 2010 (FAO 2010). As the figure below shows, the number of hungry people has increased since 1995-97... The increase has been due to three factors: 1) neglect of agriculture relevant to very poor people by governments and international agencies; 2) the current worldwide economic crisis, and 3) the significant increase of food prices in the last several years which have been devastating to those with only a few dollars a day to spend. 925 million people are 13.6 percent of the estimated world population of 6.8 billion. Nearly all of the undernourished are in developing countries.

Number of hungry people, 1969-2010

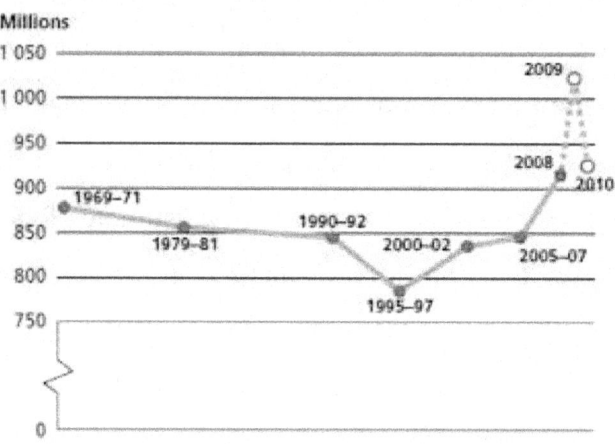

Source: FAO

In round numbers there are 7 billion people in the world. Thus, with an estimated 925 million hungry people in the world, 13.1 percent, or almost 1 in 7 people are hungry.

The FAO estimate is based on statistical aggregates. The FAO first estimates the total food supply of a country and derives the average per capita daily food intake from that. The distribution of average food intake for people in the country is then estimated from surveys measuring food expenditure. Using this information, and minimum food energy requirements, FAO estimates how many people are likely to receive such a low level of food intake that they are undernourished.[3]

Under-nutrition is a relatively new concept, but is increasingly used. It should be taken as similar to malnutrition. (It should be said as an aside, that the idea of undernourishment, its relationship to malnutrition, and the reasons for its emergence as a concept is not clear to Hunger Notes.)

Children are the most visible victims of under-nutrition. Children who are poorly nourished suffer up to 160 days of illness each year. Poor nutrition plays a role in at least half of the 10.9 million child deaths each year-five million deaths. Under-nutrition magnifies the effect of every disease, including measles and malaria. The estimated proportions of deaths in which under-nutrition is an underlying cause are roughly similar for diarrhea (61%), malaria (57%), pneumonia (52%), and measles (45%) (Black 2003, Bryce 2005). Malnutrition can also be caused by diseases, such as the diseases that cause diarrhea, by reducing the body's ability to convert food into usable nutrients.

According to the most recent estimate that Hunger Notes could find, malnutrition, as measured by stunting, affects 32.5 percent of children in developing countries--one of three. (De Onis 2000) Geographically, more than 70 percent of malnourished children live in Asia, 26 percent in Africa and 4 percent in Latin America and the Caribbean. In many cases, their plight began even before birth with a malnourished mother. Under-nutrition among pregnant women in developing countries leads to 1 out of 6 infants born with low birth weight. This is not only a risk factor for neonatal deaths, but also causes learning disabilities, mental, retardation, poor health, blindness and premature death.

Does the World Produce Enough Food to Feed Everyone?

The world produces enough food to feed everyone. World agriculture produces seventeen percent more calories per person today than it did thirty years ago, despite a seventy percent population increase. This is enough to provide everyone in the world with at least 2,720 kilocalories (kcal) per person per day according to the most recent estimate that we could find. (FAO 2002, p.9) The principal problem is that many people in the world do not have sufficient land to grow, or income to purchase, enough food.

What are the Causes of Hunger?

What are the causes of hunger is a fundamental question, with varied answers.

Poverty is the Principal Cause of Hunger.

The causes of poverty include poor people's lack of resources, an extremely unequal income distribution in the world and within specific countries, conflict and hunger itself. As of 2008

(2005 statistics), the World Bank has estimated that there were an estimated 1,345 million poor people in developing countries who live on $1.25 a day or less.[3] This compares to the later FAO estimate of 1.02 billion undernourished people. Extreme poverty remains an alarming problem in the world's developing regions, despite some progress that reduced "dollar--now $1.25-- a day" poverty from (an estimated) 1900 million people in 1981, a reduction of twenty-nine percent over the period. Progress in poverty reduction has been concentrated in Asia, and especially, East Asia, with the major improvement occurring in China. In Sub-Saharan Africa, the number of people in extreme poverty has increased. The statement that 'poverty is the principal cause of hunger' is, though correct, unsatisfying. Why then are (so many) people poor? The next section summarizes Hunger Notes answer.

Harmful Economic Systems are the Principal Cause of Poverty and Hunger.

Hunger Notes believes that the principal underlying cause of poverty and hunger is the ordinary operation of the economic and political systems in the world. Essential control over resources and income is based on military, political and economic power that typically ends up in the hands of a minority, who live well, while those at the bottom barely survive, if they do. We have described the operation of this system in more detail in our special section on harmful economic systems.

Conflict as a Cause of Hunger and Poverty:

At the end of 2005, the global number of refugees was at its lowest level in almost a quarter of a century. Despite some large-scale repatriation movements, the last three years have witnessed a significant increase in refugee numbers, due primarily to the violence taking place in Iraq and Somalia. By the end of 2008, the total number of refugees under UNHCR's mandate exceeded 10 million. The number of conflict-induced internally displaced persons (IDPs) reached some 26 million worldwide at the end of the year. Providing exact figures on the number of stateless people is extremely difficult, but relatively important. Visible though as it is, and anguishing for those involved in conflict is less important as poverty (and its causes) as a cause of hunger. (Using the statistics above 1.02 billion people suffer from chronic hunger while 36 million people are displaced [UNHCR 2008])

Hunger is also a Cause of poverty, and thus of Hunger:

By causing poor health, low levels of energy, and even mental impairment, hunger can lead to even greater poverty by reducing people's ability to work and learn, thus leading to even greater hunger.

Climate Change:

Climate change is increasingly viewed as a current and future cause of hunger and poverty. Increasing drought, flooding, and changing climatic patterns requiring a shift in crops and farming practices that may not be easily accomplished are three key issues. See the Hunger Notes special report: *Hunger, the Environment, and Climate Change* for further information, especially articles in the section: Climate change, global warming and the effect on poor people such as Global warming causes 300,000 deaths a year, study says and Could food shortages bring down civilization?

Progress in Reducing the Number of Hungry People:

The target set at the 1996 World Food Summit was to halve the number of undernourished people by 2015 from their number in 1990-92. (FAO uses three-year averages in its calculation of undernourished people.) The (estimated) number of undernourished people in developing countries was 824 million in 1990-92. In 2010, the number had climbed to 925 million people. The WFS goal is a global goal adopted by the nations of the world; the present outcome indicates how marginal the efforts were in face of the real need.

So, overall, the world is not making progress toward the world food summit goal, although there has been progress in Asia, and in Latin America and the Caribbean.

Micronutrients:

Quite a few trace elements or micronutrients--vitamins and minerals--are important for health. 1 out of 3 people in developing countries are affected by vitamin and mineral deficiencies, according to the World Health Organization. Three, perhaps the most important in terms of health consequences for poor people in developing countries, are:

Vitamin A: Vitamin A deficiency can cause night blindness and reduces the body's resistance to disease. In children, Vitamin A deficiency can also cause growth retardation. Between 100 and 140 million children are vitamins A deficient. An estimated 250,000 to 500 000 vitamin A-deficient children become blind every year, half of them dying within 12 months of losing their sight. (World Health Organization)

Iron: Iron deficiency is a principal cause of anemia. Two billion people—over 30 percent of the world's population—are anemic, mainly due to iron deficiency, and, in developing countries, frequently exacerbated by malaria and worm infections. For children, health consequences include premature birth, low birth weight, infections, and elevated risk of death. Later, physical and cognitive developments are impaired, resulting in lowered school performance. For pregnant women, anemia contributes to twenty percent of all maternal deaths. (World Health Organization)

Iodine: Iodine deficiency disorders (IDD) jeopardize children's mental health– often their very lives. Serious iodine deficiency during pregnancy may result in stillbirths, abortions and congenital abnormalities such as cretinism, a grave, irreversible form of mental retardation that affects people living in iodine-deficient areas of Africa and Asia. IDD also causes mental impairment that lowers intellectual prowess at home, at school and at work. IDD affects over 740 million people, 13 percent of the world's population. Fifty million people have some degree of mental impairment caused by IDD. (World Health Organization)

Please see the table on the following page.

(Updated December 4, 2011)

4. The table used to calculate this number.

Region	% in $1.25 a day poverty	Population (millions)	Pop. in $1 a day poverty (millions)
East Asia and Pacific	16.8	1,884	316
Latin America and the Caribbean	8.2	550	45
South Asia	40.4	1,476	596
Sub-Saharan Africa	50.9	763	388
Total Developing countries	28,8	4673	1345
Europe and Central Asia	0.04	473	17
Middle East and North Africa	0.04	305	11
Total		5451	1372

Chapter Twenty

Statistics Facts and Figures Since 2009

Most recent statistics from United Nations Food and Agriculture Organization, which was released in October 14, 2009, estimate that, " 1.2 billion people are undernourished, a sizable increase from its 2006 estimate of 854 million people. The increase has been due to three factors: 1) Neglect of agriculture relevant to very poor people by governments and international agencies. 2) The current worldwide economic crisis, and 3) The significant increase of food prices in the last several years which have been devastating to those with only a few dollars a day to spend. 1.02 billion people are 15 percent of the estimated world population of 6.8 billion. Nearly all of the undernourished are in developing countries.

The FAO estimate is based on statistical aggregates. It looks at a country's income level and income distribution and uses this information to estimate how many people receive such a low level of income that they are malnourished. It is not an estimate based on seeing to what extent actual people are malnourished and projecting from there as would be done by survey sampling.

Under-nutrition is a relatively new concept, but is increasingly used. It should be taken as basically equivalent to malnutrition. Children are the most visible victims of under-nutrition. Children who are poorly nourished suffer up to 160 days of illness each year. Poor nutrition plays a role in at least half of the 10.9 million child deaths, in which each year there are 5 million deaths. Under-nutrition magnifies the effect of every disease, including measles and malaria. The estimated proportion of deaths in which under-nutrition is an underlying cause is roughly similar for diarrhea 61%, malaria 57%, pneumonia 52% and measles 45%. (Black 2003, Bryce 2005). Malnutrition can also be caused by diseases, such as the diseases that cause diarrhea, by reducing the body's ability to convert food into usable nutrients.

According to the most recent estimate that hunger notes could find, malnutrition, is measured by stunting, affects. The percentage of children suffering from under-nutrition is a staggering 32.5% in developing countries; that's one out of three (de Onis 2000). Geographically, more than 70 percent of malnourished children live in Asia, 26 percent in Africa and 4 percent in Latin America and the Caribbean. In many cases, their plight began even before birth with a malnourished mother. Under-nutrition among pregnant women in developing countries leads to 1 out of 6 infants born with low birth weight. This is a risk factor for neonatal deaths, but also causes learning disabilities, mental, retardation, poor health, blindness and premature death.

The world produces enough food to feed everyone. World Agriculture produces 17 percent more calories per person today than it did 30 years ago, despite a 70 percent population increase. This is enough to provide everyone in the world with at least 2, 720 kilocalories (kcal) per person per day. (FAO 2002p.9) The principal problem is that many people in the world do not have sufficient land to grow, or income to purchase enough food.

The principal cause of hunger is poverty. The causes of poverty include poor people's lack of resources, an extremely unequal income distribution in the world and within specific countries, conflict, and hunger itself are issues. As of 2008, based on the (2005 statistics), the World Bank has estimated that there were an estimated 1, 345 million poor people in developing countries who live on $1.25 a day or less. This compares to the later FAO estimate of 1.02 billion undernourished people.

Extreme poverty remains an alarming problem in the world's developing regions, despite some progress that reduced "$1.25 a day" poverty from an estimated 1900 million people in 1981, a reduction of twenty-nine percent over the period. Progress in poverty reduction has been concentrated in Asia, and especially, East Asia, with the major improvement occurring in China. In Sub Sahara Africa, the number of people in extreme poverty has increased. The statement that poverty is the principal cause of hunger is, though correct, unsatisfying.

Also released is that harmful economic systems are the principal cause of poverty and hunger. Hunger notes believed that the principal underlying causes of poverty and hunger is the ordinary operation of the economic and political systems in the world. Essential control over resources and income is based on military, political and economic power that typically ends up in the hands of a minority, who live well, while those at the bottom barely survive, if they do. We have described the operation of this system in more detail in our special section on Harmful Economic systems.

Conflict as a Cause of Hunger and Poverty

At the end of 2005, the global number of refugees was at its lowest level in almost a quarter of a century. Despite some large-scale repatriation movements, the last three years have witnessed a significant increase in refugee numbers. Due primarily to the violence taking placed in Iraq and Somalia, by the end of 2008; the total number of refugees under UNHCR's mandate exceeded 10 million. The number of conflict-induced internally displaced persons (IDPs) reached some 26 million worldwide at the end of the year. Providing exact figures on the number of stateless people is extremely difficult, but relatively important; visible though as it is, and anguishing for those involved in conflict is less important as poverty (and its causes) as a cause of hunger. (Using the statistics above 1.02 billion people suffer from chronic hunger while thirty-six million people are displaced. (UNHCR 2008)

Hunger is also a cause of poverty. By causing poor health, low levels of energy and even mental impairment, hunger can lead to even greater poverty by reducing people's ability to work and learn.

Climate change is increasingly viewed as a current and future cause of hunger and poverty. Increasing drought, flooding, and changing climatic patterns requiring a shift in crops and farming practices that may not be easily accomplished are three key issues. Climate change, global warming and the effect on poor people with such a global warming causes 300,000 deaths a year, the study says and could cause food shortages that bring down civilization.

Progress in Reducing the Number of Hungry People

The target set at the 1996 World Food summit was to cut in half the number of under-nourished people by 2015 from their number in 1990-92. FAO uses three- year averages in its calculation of under-nourished people in developing countries, which was 824 million in 1990-92. In 2009, the number had climbed to 1.2 billion people. The WFS goal is a global goal adopted by the nations of the world; the present outcome indicates how marginal the efforts were in face of the real need. So, overall, the world is not making progress toward the world food summit goal, although there has been progress in Asia, in Latin America as well and the Caribbean.

According to the new estimate of September 14th, 2010 Media Center, 925 million people will suffer chronic hunger that year, while 98 million down from 1.23 billion in 2009. Hunger and malnutrition are the number one risk to the health worldwide, which imposes economic burdens on the developing world. It means 1 out of 7 people do not get enough food to be healthy in order to live an active life. Hunger and malnutrition are in fact the number one risk to the health worldwide; this is greater than Aids,

Malaria and Tuberculosis. The major causes of hunger are natural disaster, conflict, poverty, poor agricultural infrastructure and over-exploitation of the environment. Financial and economic crises moved people to the state of hunger. This still continues up until this present moment.

Conclusion

With this valuable information: I urge the leaders of the nations, to fight the war of hunger, disease, death, poverty, economic crisis and malnutrition in order to preserve the welfare and health of the next generation. They need to spend money and make all efforts to help the nations that are suffering from hunger, lack of medical treatment and medical supplies. It should not be the problem of United Nation alone; it should be the responsibility of all the nations in the world. They need to spend money where money is needed to be spent. Instead of spending money on war that has no end, while millions of children are dying of hunger and malnutrition and lack of medical care, the world leaders must remember the children and help them. They are going to be the next generation of the people in the world. We must make sure that they are in good health and that they are functioning very well. The soldiers can help FAO to take the food to the people instead of handing them over to the political government where distribution is limited, not general, or based on whom you know. We see

Three Solutions for World Peace

thousands of Haitian people still sleeping in tents and in temporary shelter since the earthquake in January of 2010. According to the news report, billions of dollars was given to the government of Haiti, but we don't know what happened to it. The children continue to suffer and all manner of abuse happen with them everyday in the tents.

In addition, educational systems need to be built for the school age children, young adults and adult alike. They should use the money that would have been spent on war, applied it with all their efforts and attention into a 5-year program. All nations should continue to help the countries in Asia and the African continents to solve the war of hunger, war of lack of energy, lack of food, water, medical needs that face these people everyday. The Chinese proverb says: "Give me a fish and I eat for a day. Teach me to fish and I eat fish for life."

The Bible says: "When the Son of Man comes in His glory, and all the angels with Him, He will sit on is throne in heavenly glory. All the nations will be gathered before Him, and He will divide people one from another as a shepherd separates the sheep from the goats. He will put the sheep on his right and the goats on his left. Then the King will say to those on his right. Come, you who are blessed by my Father, take your inheritance, the kingdom prepared for you since the creation of the world. For I was hungry and you gave me something to eat, I was thirsty and you gave me something to drink, I was a stranger and you invited me in, I needed clothes and you clothed me, I was sick and you looked after me, I was in prison and you came to visit me. Then the righteous will answer him, Lord, when did we see you hungry and feed you, or thirsty and give you something to drink? When did we see you a stranger and invite you in or needing clothes and clothe you? When did we see you sick or in prison and go to visit you? The King will reply, I tell you the truth, whatever you did for one of the least of these brothers of mine, and you did for me.

Then He will say to those on his left. Depart from me, you who are cursed, into the eternal fire prepared for the devil and his angels. For I was hungry and you gave me nothing to eat, I was thirsty and you gave me nothing to drink. I was a stranger and you did not invite me in. I needed clothes and you did not clothe me. I was sick and in prison and you did not look after me. They also will answer, Lord, when did we see you hungry or thirsty or a stranger or needing clothes or sick, or in prison, and did not help you? He will reply, I tell you the truth, whatever you did not do for one of the least of these, you did not do for me." (Mathew 25:31-45)

What the Bible is telling us is that, at the time of Christ's coming, the saved and the lost that are living on Earth and who survived the Tribulation, will still live and mingle together. Christ appearing to judge the world will be splendid and glorious. Christ will come to the judgment seat in real glory and all the people in the world shall see what the Saints only do now believe that he is the brightness of his Father's glory. Christ's second coming will be in a great bright cloud of glory. When Christ comes in his glory to judge the world, he will bring all his holy angels with him. There will be an appearing of all the children of men before him, he will gather all the nations before him. The judgment of that great day will be a general judgment. All those nations of men that are made of one blood, to dwell on all the face of the Earth shall be summoned before Christ.

The judgment will involve the separation of the wicked from the righteous. Those who are doing good by helping the poor and the needy, people who need food, clothing, helping the homeless people in the world, who need shelter to sleep, water to drink; and the sick that are in need of medical and all types of various medical treatment. Therefore, the judgment will be based on outward works of love and kindness to those belonging to Christ to those who are suffering in the world.

The expression of love and compassion is taken as an inherent part of true faith and salvation. This is why the second great commandment is to love our brothers, our neighbors and everyone in the world. We must give the proof of the love by our readiness to do well to others, help those who are in need of help, and to communicate good wishes. Give to those who have not; works of charity and beneficence, according to our ability as necessary, they must show mercy to those who are in need of a cup of mercy at all times; those good works shall then be accepted which are done in the name of the Lord Jesus Christ.

I urge the nations to stop fighting war civil war within the nation or war between two nations. The world leaders should be thinking of doing well to other nations that are in need of help. As we do not know when Christ will return to judge the nations. They must look for any means to help other nations so that their people will not die everyday of disease, lack of water, lack of food and, especially, lack of medical care.

Let it be clear to them that there will be no perfect peace in any nation of the world until the Prince of Peace returns. Jesus Christ is the Blessed Ruler of all the souls of human beings on the Earth. I resolved all into the sovereignty of God as Apostle Paul did, "Oh, the depth of the riches of the wisdom and knowledge of God. How unsearchable His judgments and His paths beyond tracing out. Who has known the mind of the Lord? Or who has been His counselor? Who has ever given to God, that God should repay him? For from Him, and through Him, and to Him, are all things; To Him be the glory forever Amen." (Roman 11:33-36 NIV) God is rich in mercy, love, grace, faithfulness, power, and goodness. His wisdom is infinite, unsearchable, incomparable, incomprehensible and invincible.

God is full of knowledge and He is omniscient. He knows everything: everything is possible for everything is actual; all the events on Earth, all the creatures, of the past, present, and future are under His control and under His command. His decisions are unsearchable: they are too deep for mortal minds to fully understand or comprehend, the ways in which He arranges creation, history, redemption and providence are beyond our limited comprehension. There is no created being that can know the mind of the Lord, except whom He chooses to reveal it. No one is qualified to advise God. He doesn't need our counsel and wouldn't profit by it. He is the source of every good thing. He is the active agent in sustaining and controlling the Universe, and He is the object for which everything has been created. Everything is designed to bring great glory to His holy name. That is, God is all in all. God is the spring and fountain of all, through Christ, as the conveyance, God is the ultimate end. If everything that is going on in the world were of Him and through Him, the people of this world should be to Him and for Him. Whether we like it or not, all creation shall be in the end to Him. In this verse Apostle Paul expresses his awe of God and of the profound and humanly incomprehensible wisdom and judgments of God in redemptive history. What else can be said, than to say that, "To Him be the glory forever." Amen, Amen, Amen.

Three Solutions for World Peace

Chapter Twenty-One

Conclusion

Upon reviewing all these violent wars and killings in the world, it comes to me clearly that people of the world are missing one important point that holds lives and liberty together. Without these three words that must start right from day one when an individual is born, that is automatically transferred from the parents to the newborn child, which will grow with the child everyday until he or she becomes an adult and uses it, practices it and manifests it to other people around them. It is the teaching of our Lord Jesus Christ during His earthly ministry. Jesus Christ said to the people as they followed Him, listened to His teaching everyday, and learned from His great teachings and parables.

Christ said, "Love Thy Neighbor" this is the love that all the religions of the world preach, but they do not practice it, or use it in any of their daily involvement with themselves and with others. These three words begins from your household, from the people in your building to your neighborhood, then to people in your community, continues with the people in the entire city, state and branches out to everyone in our nation, which will expand to all the people in the entire world. Your question now to me is- how does this, or how can this solve the violence and killing in the world? If you are a Muslim you must love your God Allah, and love yourself, do unto others, as you want others to do unto you. If you practice this again and again every day you will apply it to the people in your household, your office and in your place of worship. Love and kindness will then spread to everyone around you. If everyone around you started the same thing for one year it will be part of them and it will continue to spread to the entire neighborhood from one person to another and it will spread to everyone in the neighborhood; before you know it, it will spread to the entire city from everyone in the city of New York for example.

We will love each other, think good of each other and offer help for those who are in need of help. Correct those who are doing wrong with love not by violence. When someone drives pass you inappropriately, you will not curse, but just correct with love. If someone accuses you wrongly, you will take your time to explain to him or her, with the spirit of understanding, to a confused brother in a conflict that will then end in peace. If this continues throughout the city, it will spread to the people in the state.

If it continues throughout the states, peace will be manifest gradually among the people, the next generation of children will be growing up with love; they will be learning how to return good for evil and pray for their enemy. The number of people suffering with high blood pressure will be reduced, those who are suffering from heart diseases will be reduced because they have peace within themselves at all times. This is as if one is trying to lose weight and states within himself and practices to eat less food everyday; the result started gradually until everybody sees clearly that this person has lost a lot of weight. So is someone who practices everyday to love their neighbor. When this happens and continues, the entire nations will live in peace and other nations around them will join. The land is always there; there is no reason why thousands of people have to die because of a piece of land.

A dictator that does not want to leave his position must realize that the world is temporary, that he is going to grow old and die. The Bible says that God gave us His Spirit and we became a living being. When He takes away His Spirit, we become dust and die and are gone forever.

Three Solutions for World Peace

A dictator of any country must know that one day they will go back to dust. When the people who elected them in that position tell them to leave, they should leave with love and without violence. If they leave the position with love, life will be preserved and countries will be stable with no destruction of houses and properties. The dictator will continue to enjoy his or her life without interruption in his country or in another country. Again, with love the people, such as police and military, which their duty is to protect, the people in their country will not have to kill anyone. These people contradict themselves and turn their duty around by listening to one person that is ordering them to kill their own brothers and sisters. If there is love within the country, in the heart and mind of every individual in the country, there will be no violence, no killing and no suicide bombings. If one nation can be strong enough to practice how to love their neighbor, the entire people in other countries will join them.

If every person, in every nation, can love each other for one year, in two years it wills continually be said that no nation will fight another nation or plan to destroy other nations.

We know that there will be no perfect peace until the Prince of Peace returns to the Earth. In the Book of Isaiah 2:3-4, "Jesus Christ the King of kings the Lord of lords, the God of Gods the only Ruler of all souls in the Universe who is the source of peace." Peace lives in the heart where God's Spirit dwells; when everyone in the world practices love with each other, the Spirit of God will dwell in the heart; they will learn and practice how to live in peace starting with their children, husband, wives, siblings, neighbors, friends, coworkers, including college students in the dormitory. The people of the world will live in peace with each other; all the people in all the nations will continue to learn, search for principles and values that bring peace, good lives and social economic stability to all the people in the world.

There will be an increase as we are going in unity among the nations. There will be unity among the people of different religions and the peoples of every different religion. With love, they will know that there is only one God, the creator of Heaven and Earth, the sea and everything that dwells in it. All will know that Jesus Christ is the Son of God that is full of truth, grace and the Holy Spirit and that they are forever one God.

God, whom in Him we move, eat, sleep, wake and walk around, in Him we have our being. Christians will sit comfortably in the Jewish Synagogues; Christians and Jewish alike will worship together in the mosque; Hindus and Buddhists will worship with Christians, Muslims and Jewish people without problems or violence because everyone on Earth will have one spirit, the Spirit of God ruling and directing every human being's soul, spirit and body. This is when the word, "United Nations" will have an effect and when the world leaders say anything, there will be no opposition because the world leaders will operate with love.

This will be when they operate with the Spirit of God indwelling within them, people will listen to them and there will be peace, but not perfect peace until Christ returns with a new Earth where righteousness will dwell forever. Our Lord said, "God is a Spirit. Those who worship him must worship Him in Spirit and in truth." The Spirit is like a wind you heard the sound and its activities such as a hurricane, but you do not know where it is coming from or where it's going. Thus it is the same with the people that God's Spirit indwells within them; they are full of love just as God is love and no unrighteousness is in Him. "For God so loved the world that he gave his only begotten Son, that whosoever believeth in him should not perish, but have everlasting life." (Jn. 3:16) This verse reveals the heart and the purpose of God, the Father and Almighty, in the lives of His people.

God's love is wide enough to embrace all the people of the world. God gave his Son as an offering for sin on the Cross. The full peace of God is just the peace of God that surpasses all understanding. They cannot think of any violence or killing if they seek the peace of God at all times. They sleep in peace and wake-up in peace, the peace of God rules their heart, mind and spirit. They are full of joy at all times because there is not any form of evil thinking in their hearts. Therefore, they are full of joy all the days of their lives. When the Spirit of God dwells in the heart, the people or a person, the love of God overflows to everyone around that person. The person will be full of happiness that his or life impacts someone and changes their lives from any form of evil to love, from hatred to love, from violence to love, from wickedness to love and from jealousy to love.

Some people have a spirit of jealousy, which ruins the lives of people around them. Helping others will help you to be a good leader in the community, city, state, nation and in the world. The Creator, God, will guarantee the future world of peace.

"But in the last days it shall come to pass, that the mountain of the house of the Lord shall be established in the top of the mountains, and it shall be exalted above the hills; and people shall flow unto it. And many nations shall come, and say, 'Come, and let us go up to the mountain of the Lord, and to the house of the God of Jacob; and he will teach us of his ways, and we will walk in his paths', for the law shall go forth of Zion, and the world of the Lord from Jerusalem. And he shall judge among many people, and rebuke strong nations afar off; and they shall beat their swords into plowshares, and their spears into pruning hooks: nation shall not lift up a sword against nation; neither shall they learn war any more. But they shall sit every man under his wine and under his fig tree; and none shall make them afraid: for the mouth of the Lord of hosts hath spoken it. For all people will walk everyone in the name of his god, and we will walk in the name of the Lord our God for ever and ever." (Mic. 4:1-4)

The Prophet Micah prophesies that there will be a time when God will rule over the entire world. And it will be a time of peace, happiness and godliness. God will be honored and worshiped not only by Israel, but also by all the people in all the nations of the world. The mountain of the Lord's temple in Jerusalem will be the center of God's government. This future Kingdom of God will begin when Christ returns to destroy all evil and to establish His righteous reign on Earth. We are God's voice of truth and His messenger on the Earth, let godliness and righteousness prevail. Leaders of the world must rule with love and peace.

"Because that, when they know God, they glorified him not as God, neither were thankful; but became vain in their imaginations, and their foolish heart was darkened. Professing themselves to be wise, they became fools." (Rm. 1:21-22)

Leaders of the nations, either a dictator or a liberal leader, must know that they cannot live on this Earth forever; they should remember that one day death will arrive and they will be gone forever. For example, the Egyptian era is gone, the Greek era is gone, the Napoleon Era is gone, the Roman Empire era is gone, the British Era is gone, Hitler has died and is gone forever.

With this in mind, leaders should stop killing their own people, including their own children, just because they wanted to continue to stay in power. There is no power, but the power of God. Leaders that make the army and police to kill people that vote them into power must realized that they will die one day and face the judgment of God. When a leader sits down, eats, sleeps and play cards while thousands of his people are being killed every minute on the street, that leader shows himself as an evil person. If he truly loves his people, he will not order them to be killed.

The Bible says, "And the Lord God formed man of the dust of the ground, and breathed into his nostrils the breath of life; and man became a living soul." (Gen. 2:7) These words speak to the entire human race to have complete dependence on God, not on any image, not on philosophical experience and not on any work of human hands.

We need to remember what happened in the world, which affected all the nations from 1930 -1940 and part of the Holocaust of World War II, which was part of every nation. These are all part of world history that can never be erased. Since then, every nation that has kicked out God, has failed. God is the judge of human race; the time of judgment has been determined and it will be executed through a man that God raised from the dead.

God breathed into our nostrils the breath of life means that He gave us life. Human beings were created in a special way different from the animals. God gave us His Spirit, an eternal Spirit, which always exists until He takes it away from us. We must know that there is a world beyond ours that we are unable to see, but it does exist. Our Spirit is reaching out to God, the Creator.

We are a spirit beings; our spirit is connected to God's spirit. If our spirit ceases to connect to God's spirit we die and are gone forever from this current world. Money cannot buy death; positional power cannot buy death; no medical treatment, no medication, no science can buy death. All the political leaders of the world must plan to think about love and peace of the people of their country and for other nations.

One day death is going to knock on the door of their heart. Their spirit from God is going to leave and they go back to dust. God breathed into us a spirit that came directly from His own Spirit. This is the reason why we are different from the animals. We became living souls. (Job 32:8)

It is this spirit that enables us to live as a human being, made us and gives us life. We die when the Spirit of God leaves our body; nothing can revive us and no mouth to mouth resuscitation would have any effect because the spirit already went back to the owner. When our spirit leaves our body, we return to the ground and become dust. This means that God gave us His Spirit. We became a living being, then, when He takes away His Spirit, we become dust and return to dust to die and are gone forever.

On the day of Jesus Christ's crucifixion, our Lord said, "Father, into thy hands I commend my spirit." (Lk.23:46) Stephen, one of Jesus' disciple, when he was stoned to death before he died he said, "And they stoned Stephen, call upon [God], and saying, 'Lord Jesus, receive my spirit.'" (Acts 7:59) It is the same with everyone on this planet Earth. There will be a time when, whether they like it or not, that the spirit will go back to the Creator. At that moment, everyone that said there is no God, will see and know clearly that there is one true God; only they cannot come back and tell us. We people on this Earth are like a robot, a computer, or any other machinery controlled by some power that is programmed within them. When that power is gone, the robot will not be able to walk. It is the same with human beings; the spirit helps us to function, but when Spirit of God is gone from the body, it is useless.

All the people in power should read this book and change from hatred to love, from wickedness to love and from violence to peace. Let love prevail; let us love ourselves and our neighbor; let us love people in our country and let us love everybody in the world. Let us live together with love, which is the bond of peace. Peace be unto all on the Earth. We will all look forward to the peace and reconciliation that only the Messiah, the Lord Jesus Christ, the Son of God can bring to the Middle East, North Africa and the entire world when He returns. Christ gave us the parable of the man that fell upon the thieves on the road to Jericho, a Samaritan shows a passion of love. (Lk 10:30-37)

We should do the same on this Earth to others to have peace in the entire nations of Earth. The act of love and compassion for others in our nation and for people in other nations will spread. The billions of dollars wasted on wars and terrorist attacks should have been spent in the countries where there is no rain, no water, no food and should be used to help people and

Three Solutions for World Peace

children that are dying everyday from lack. Support should go where a mother cannot give a name to her child until after four years of age for fear that the child might die before the age of four years old due to lack of water, food and shelter.

A bowel of compassion and love should come from oil rich countries to spend on the suffering neighboring countries around them. Instead of building nuclear weapons against each other, nations let us promote love and build love, using the money for water, energy and sustainable projects around the world. Many people around us are dying of hunger; tons of tons of food from the public schools around the nation in America are thrown away everyday.

Some children suffer from obesity because they eat too much in school and at home. One seven year old asked me one day when I visited him in the school very early in the morning; he said to me, "Why do they have to eat breakfast in the school? Why can't we just come to school and exercise in the gym for thirty minutes or sing a song?" The child said that his mother forced him to eat before he left home everyday and his friend in school forced him to eat breakfast with him again. The child said by the time he got to the class, he always feels sleepy; he can hardly keep his eyes open and he always gets in trouble with his teacher for sleeping in the class. I explained to the child that breakfast is for the kids that do not have the opportunity to eat at home before coming to the school, whereas it is the responsibility of the parents to feed their kids before leaving home in the morning. The child said that lots of food goes to the garbage because some kids do not eat. In this case, research is needed to find out how such food could be preserved and shipped to the poor children in other parts of the world where there is no food and water, no crops coming out, no clothing and no shelter.

It is time to live with love with each other and plan how to help each other. It is time now to make other people comfortable in there own country. According to the news, "600,000 Haitian earthquake victims are still living in the tents after the earthquake that destroyed half of the nation." Instead of fighting people from all over the countries, the nations should gather together and find out how to build houses for themselves faster than what their political systems are doing. Other countries that have no disasters suffer from lack of water, energy and medical supplies.

If all the nations lived together with love, all this help could have been given for those who are in desperate need of help in the appropriate manner and time. The world would be at peace and in peace with their neighboring countries if the world leaders could develop solutions of how to help other nations who are in need of help, instead of fighting, bombing and the planning of terrorist attacks that never stop and that have no meaning.

The terrorists have no love for their own people. Bound up with bombs, children as little as 9, 10 and 15 years old carry out suicide bombings. They destroy their own children, their own people to do evil because they have no love for them. My question is, when are they going to realize that a destroyer is destroying *them* by using their own children to carry out suicide bombing operations. They have no love for the mother and father or those children that they are using to carry out suicide bombing operations.

I pray that God will reveal himself to the terrorists and let them know what they are doing to their own people everyday when there are suicide bombing attacks. The Lord is saying that the blood of those people that the terrorists are using to kill thousands of people and the innocent people that die every day in terrorist attacks is crying out to Him in Heaven and there is going to be a day of judgment for the terrorist people on this Earth. And that day is coming soon, because God will not let wickedness continue forever without punishment.

Therefore, I urge all the terrorists to stop their operations and come forward to let the United Nations know what is it they need before they kill all their children by using them for suicide bombings. Terrorists should stop all their terrorist actions in the world and live in peace and love with people in the world. I see the terrorist actions as complete acts of wickedness, not to the people in the world, but to themselves, their children, their wives and to everyone that live with them. These operations are characterized as a lack of love and there is not one single one of them that has love in them. They live with violence, plan evil; they sleep and wake-up everyday of their lives with the plan of evil in their hearts towards other people when they are use suicide bombings towards other people in the world. Al-Qaeda and the Taliban, wherever they are, need to think seriously and come to the conclusion that they must stop their terrorist actions and live lives of peace and love.

Love is the main thing that can hold the people in the world together. Love is the key to a peaceful life. Love is the beginning of lives and love will be the end of this life when Christ returns. When we love ourselves we will be able to love others and we will be able to look out for the good of others. We would be able to think good and eat good, sharing the love of God that brings peace and good harmony to everyone and to all the nations.

Love is the bond of peace in this world; none can achieve peace without love; nothing can and there is nothing that can bring peace to the world other than love. That is why Jesus Christ taught us to love our neighbor, pray for those who hate you, do good to those who do bad to you. Return evil that others did to you with good; return hatred with love. Love is the bond of peace perfected and that will make Jesus Christ to return to this Earth to judge the quick and the dead and the all the eyes shall see Him.

That same love will make Him to bless us with a new Heaven and a new Earth where only righteousness will dwell, where animals will be running around playing with the children. There will be no war, no dictators, no presidents, no United Nations, everyone will live in perfect peace with each other. As the scripture says, "One Lord, one faith, one baptism, one God and Father of all, who is over all and through all and in all." (Eph. 4:5)

"And many people shall go and say, come ye, and let us go up to the mountain of the Lord, to the house of the God of Jacob, and he will teach us of his ways, and we will walk in his paths, for out of Zion shall go forth the law, and the world of the Lord from Jerusalem. And he shall Judge among the nations, and shall rebuke many people; and they shall beat their swords into plows shares, and their spears into pruning hooks: nations shall not life up sword against nations, neither shall they learn war anymore." (Is 2:4) What this Old Testament Scripture is saying, is that this last day period between the first and second comings of Christ, are what the Prophet Isaiah describes how the complete fulfillment of this Scripture will be at Christ's second coming, when God's kingdom will be established on Earth.

The Prophet Isaiah prophesies of a time when God's rule will be established over all the Earth. All evil, injustice and rebellion directed against God and his law will be put down and righteousness will reign. All nations will worship and serve the Lord. The Prophet Isaiah's prophecy reflects God's final purpose for Israel and all the human race. Part of this prophecy was fulfilled through Jesus Christ during His earthly ministry where he executed justice and righteousness here on Earth. Isaiah's prophecy speaks of a coming deliverer who would one day lead the people of God to joy, peace, righteousness and justice; this person is the Messiah, who is Jesus Christ and the Son of God.

Isaiah's prophecy reveals several important truths about the coming Messiah. The primary concern of all who come to the Lord should be to know and to obey God's will as citizens of His Kingdom. It is very important for those who proclaim God's message to take supreme care that their preaching and teaching are the correct words of God based on the inspired Word of God from the Scriptures as revealed through Jesus Christ, the Old Testament Prophets and the New Testament Apostles. All people, both the lost and the saved, need to hear God's truth proclaimed from the lips of those anointed by the Holy Spirit and those that are committed to righteousness in light of God's ways. "But in the last days it shall come to pass, that the mountain of the house of the Lord shall be established in the top of the mountains, and it shall be exalted above the hills, and people shall flow unto it. And many nations shall come, and say, come, and let us go up to the mountain of the Lord, and to the house of the God of Jacob, and he will teach us of his ways, and we will walk in His path: for the law shall go forth of Zion, and the word of the Lord from Jerusalem. And he shall judge among many people, and rebuke strong nations into plowshares, and their spears into pruning hoods: Nations shall not lift up a sword against nation; neither shall they learn war any more. But they shall sit every man under his vine and under his fig tree; and none shall make them afraid: for the mouth of the Lord of Host hath spoken it."(Is. 2:2-3)

Again Prophet Micah prophesies a time when God will rule over the entire world. There is going to be a time of peace, happiness and godliness; God will be honored and worshiped by all the people in the world. The Mountain of the Lord's Temple Jerusalem will be the center of God's government. This means that the Kingdom of God will begin when Jesus Christ returns to put a stop to all the evils in the world and establishes His righteous reign on Earth.

Three Solutions for World Peace

Luke 10:30-37 says, "Jesus Christ was teaching and preaching during His earthly ministry, someone in the crowed wanted to justify himself and asked Jesus, 'And who is my neighbor?' Jesus answered and said, 'A certain man went down from Jerusalem to Jericho, and fell among thieves which stripped him of his raiment, and wounded him, and departed, leaving him half dead. And by chance there came down a certain priest that way; and when he saw him, he passed by on the other side. And likewise a Levite, when he was at the place, came and looked on him, and passed by on the other side. But a certain Samaritan, as he journeyed, came where he was: and when he saw him, he had compassion on him, and went to him, and bound up his wounds, pouring in oil and wine, and set him on his own beast, and brought him to an inn, and took care of him. And on the morrow when he departed, he took out two pence, and gave them to the host, and said unto him, take care of him, and whatsoever thou spendest more, when I come again, I will repay thee. Which now of these three thinkest thou, was a neighbor unto him that fell among the thieves? And he said, 'He that showed mercy on him.' The said Jesus unto him, " 'Go and do likewise.'" (Lk.10:30-37)

The parable of our Lord is directed to all the people in the world then, as well as all the people in the world today. The parable emphasizes that true saving faith and obedience is compassion for those who are in need. We must love God our creator and we are to love our neighbor and other people around us. This is the new life and the gift of grace that Christ gives to those who believe in Him to produce love, mercy and compassion for those who are distressed and afflicted.

It is the responsibility of all believers to act on the Holy Spirit's love within them and not to harden their hearts. As true believers and other people of different religions, we must not harden our hearts by being insensitive to the suffering and needs of others. Our neighbors are those who need us when it is in our power to help them. We must be active in the service of God. This service is essential and good.

Our first and most important task is love and devotion that expresses itself in quiet worship, with prayer and fellowship with the Lord. As we serve the Lord by performing good deeds we must not forget that the first and greatest commandment is to love the Lord our God with our whole hearts, all our soul with all our strength body and minds. As we love the Lord we will be able to go to prayer. Jesus said, "God is Spirit and they that worship Him must worship Him in Spirit and in truth." (Jn 4:24)

Jesus Christ points to the level at which true worship happens. We must come to God in complete sincerity and with a spirit that is directed by the life and the activity of the Holy Spirit. While truth characterized as the attribute of God, incarnate in Christ, it is intrinsic to the Holy Spirit. Therefore, worship must take place according to the truth of the Father that is revealed in the Son and received through the Spirit. Worship in spirit and truth in Jesus Christ is the to live in union with Christ. This requires speaking the truth to have fellowship with Christ and to possess salvation, yet to live and speak according to the truth.

To be deceived is to live with darkness and outside the kingdom of Heaven. We must live in truth in love and in compassion with one another, speaking the truth in love. This is the best solution for the world peace. "You shall love your neighbor as yourself." (Mark 12:28-31) Jesus Christ was a great teacher and preacher during his earthly ministry and still is today. Christ is telling us that our relationship, fellowship our association with our family, children, co-workers and other people in the world is inseparable from our relationship with God. There should be no difference. God created us in his own image.

The love of God and our love for our neighbor are the two keys to life. All the people of this world are God's people. God required them to love each other including their enemies. Love for God is the first and greatest commandment. Therefore, in our practice to love one another and love all the people in the world no matter what they are, what lifestyle they are in, whether they are Christian, Muslim, Buddhist, Hindus, idol worshipers, Atheists, or a follower of any other religion of the world, no matter what color of their skin, we must love them; we must never compromise the supremacy of our love for God and the righteous standards of His Word. Jesus' word of teaching still is directed against all religious leaders and teachers, Rabbi, Imam and all other religious leaders of the world, who had rejected the true Word of God and replaced it with their own ideas and their own interpretations. Jesus said, " A new command I give you: love one another as I have loved you, so you must love one another. By this all men will know that you are my disciples, if you love one another." (Jn.13:34-35)

Loving all the people in the world, including those who are not Christian, or Muslim, does not mean that we must compromise or accommodate our particular biblical beliefs or doctrinal differences. The love for God and His will as revealed in His Word must control and direct our love for other people of the world.

Let's talk about who our neighbor is. Many people think that their neighbor is based only on someone living in the same building, same floor, same street or the same gated community. Jesus said that it could be someone you only saw once, or at that particular moment, or someone you just met at the side of the road.

Jesus means all the human beings, all the living souls, all mankind, including all our enemies; He gave us a parable of the Good Samaritan to make His teaching clear to the people of His day and to us today. "Love your Neighbor. . ." means, love all the people in your country and in all the nations of the world. This parable speaks to us thoroughly about what we are and what is going on in our world. The Jews and Samaritans were enemies of each other even before Jesus; they considered Samaritans unclean, outcasts and not religious. The Samaritan is the one that helped the wounded man. We are the same today. We feel that some people are not religious; that we are better than them. They are atheists, Muslims, Hindus, Buddhists, idol worshipers, same sex-marriage partners, African, Chinese or Spanish. We always feel that we are superior than the other person, so we distance ourselves.

Therefore, as long as we are still breathing on this planet, we must love one another. Love is the bond of peace in the world. Love is the only thing that can bring perfect peace to all the people all the nations in the world. Let us begin today to practice how to love one another. "Love your enemies. . ." (Lk. 6:27-38) Jesus said that an unforgiving heart is full of hatred, which easily blocks the love of God, beginning from parents, children, adult children, between husbands and wives, friends, co-workers, as well as between the nations. When there is no love between the nations they plan war, revenge for any wrong between them and waste human lives.

Please understand those that have no love for each other, kill and destroy each other. They plan any form of evil against each other, against the neighboring countries and against other people who have different religious beliefs. They plan evil all the time to destroy those who do not have the same religious beliefs. Such people lack the love for God and cause violence and death. Even if they pray 3, 4 or 5 times, even 7 times a day, it does not have any effect on their heart because the God they call they do not love Him. There is no true God that would tell anyone to kill other created beings in order to get to Heaven. God is love; there is no righteousness, except in Him.

People of the world and religious leaders turned the Bible, the Qur'an and all other religions' holy books around for their own purpose and their own wickedness; they gave different interpretations of the Word of God. God is the God of all people in all the nations of the world. He cannot change and He has never changed. God is a God of mercy; His mercy endures forever and ever. God wants us to come to Him in so many ways, in so many languages, in so many forms because He is the creator, the Blessed Ruler of all the souls of human beings. God is a great God above all other Gods; Jesus Christ, His only begotten Son and Holy Spirit are forever one God. Whatever we do not understand in regards to the attributes of God, in all His Holiness we must leave it alone and ask that question or we will automatically find out when we die and leave this Earth.

Jesus tells us how we are to live with other persons, loving our enemies does not mean an emotional love, such as liking our enemies, but rather a genuine concern for their good and for their eternal salvation. God wants us to repay good for evil that people do to us. Loving our enemies does not mean standing by and doing nothing, while the evil doers continue their wickedness. When it is necessary for God's honor, the good or safety of others, or the ultimate good of the wicked, severe action must be taken to stop evil.

Our heart is the center of our being, it determines our outward behavior. It must be regenerated and must be changed in order for us to possess the mind of God and the love of God that will flow like a river to other people in the world.

God wants us to serve others with our gift and talents He created in us. We can use all our resources and gifts talents to help others. For example, people with the gift of encouragement, dance, mercy and sports help others to enjoy life, to laugh and to be happy. We can give donated money to some charitable organizations to help those who are sick and lonely. We can do humanitarian work through the United Nations in a country where they are in need of help. We can do voluntary work in our city, states and in the hospitals. We can be peacemakers and ambassadors for peace in the world. We can decide to do our jobs as a duty of respect and as a gift to God, doing God's work truthfully and sincerely. Doctors, lawyers, clerks, policeman, politicians, bank tellers, CEOs, if we know that what we do we do for the glory of God, we will do our daily duty with the love of God.

Serving others truthfully will help our lives to be full of joy and fulfillment, good health, power and wealth. We will be able to solve all our problems without worries. We will be able to live in the fullness of the goodness of God. Every one of us must be able to give generously the gift of love. If we want to be full of God's love everyday, we must learn how to love all the people in the world because they are His people. Loving your neighbor is the opposite of selfishness. Selfishness is the common human practice. When we love God with all our heart, soul, mind and strength, we grow to recognize that everyone is part of His creation. Owe no one anything, except to love one another, for he or she who loves one another has fulfilled the law. Therefore, love is the fulfillment of the Law. Love thy neighbors means respect for others and to have regard for their needs and desires as highly as we regard ourselves. The key is to recognize who is our neighbor.

Who is our neighbor? Again, it might be the woman that screamed and yelled at her dog, the bank teller that asked you a silly question about your money in your account, your pastor and assistant pastor in your church who always tell you what to do and what not to do as a school teacher would; they are all someone that God values and loves, just as He loves you.

Jesus Christ came to save us by pardoning us from our past, present and future sins. God so loved the world that He gave his only, begotten Son. Jesus Christ is the only begotten Son of God. Because of His sacrifice on the Cross, man may receive the redemption and salvation through Him; it pleased God to give His only begotten Son. He gave His best, that is, He gave Him up to suffer and die for us. His enemies could not have taken Him if His Father had not given Him up as a sacrificial offering to the world. Herein God commended His love to the world. God so loved the world, so thoroughly and richly.

Let us think and wonder that a great God should love such a worthless world; that the Holy God should love such a wicked world; Jews believed that the Messiah would be sent in love to their nation only; but Jesus Christ tells them that he came in love to the whole world, to all the inhabitants of the world, to Gentiles as well as Jews.

Through our Lord Jesus Christ there is a general offer of life and salvation made to all. "God so loved the world that He sent His Son with this proposal, that whosoever believes in Him shall not perish, but have everlasting life." (John 3:16) Jesus Christ is known as the only means to salvation to the ends of the Earth.

God became flesh and lived among people at Nazareth in a Galilean neighborhood for thirty-three years. The people of His days saw Him with their very own eyes. The glory that never fades away; glory of the Father to the Son, the true God, the very God; Who is, and who was, and who is to come, eternal, unchangeable, He is before the throne; for as God made, so he governs, all things by His Spirit; Son forevermore.

The Word of God is alive and living inside everyone in the world. We have to try our best to keep peace in the world until the Prince of Peace returns. We shall behold Him as the one who was crucified, coming back from Heaven with a great light and with all the archangels. People of the world will be very happy and rejoice upon His return, his name is Wonderful Counselor, for He is both

God and man. He is the counselor for he was intimately acquainted with the counsels of God from eternity and he gives counsel to the children of men. He is the wisdom of the Father and is made of God to give us wisdom. He is the mighty God, with great wisdom and strength. He is able to save to the utmost; He is the everlasting Father or the Father of Eternity; He is God, who is one with the Father, who is from everlasting to everlasting. He is the author of everlasting life and happiness to all. He is the Prince of Peace as a King, he preserves, commands and creates peace in His kingdom. He is our peace. His throne is above every throne.

"And the government will be on His shoulders. And He will be called Wonderful Counselor, Mighty God, Everlasting Father and Prince of Peace. Of the increase of His government and peace there will be no end. He will reign on David's throne and over his kingdom, establishing and upholding it with justice and righteousness from that time on and forever. The zeal of the Lord Almighty will accomplish this." (Isaiah 9:6b-7)

"He shall bear the burden of every nation. There shall be a peaceable government, agreeable to His character as the Prince of Peace. He shall rule with love, and as His government increases the peace shall increase. He shall rule with righteousness, peace with God for humankind through deliverance from sin and death, justice and judgment, it shall be an everlasting kingdom.

He will not judge by what he sees with his eyes, or decide by what he hears with his ears; but with righteousness he will judge the needy, with justice he will give decisions for the poor of the Earth. He will strike the earth with the rod of his mouth; with the breath of his lips he will slay the wicked. Righteousness will be his belt and faithfulness the sash around his waist. The wolf will live with the lamb, the leopard with lie down with the goat, the calf and the lion and the yearling together; and a little child will lead them.

The cow will feed with bear, their young will lie down together, and the lion will eat straw like the ox. The infant will play near the hole of the cobra, and the young child put his hand into viper's nest. Neither will neither barn nor destroy on all my holy mountain, for the earth will be full of the knowledge of the Lord as the water covers the sea. He will raise a banner for the nations." (Isaiah 11:3b-9, 12) There shall be no end of the increase of His government. The Lord of hosts, who has all power in his hand and all creatures at his command, shall accomplish this.

Jesus was summing up all the law in these two statements: "You have heard that it was said, Love your neighbor and hate your enemy, but I tell you Love your enemies and pray for those who persecute you, that you may be sons of your Father in Heaven.

He causes His sun to rise on the evil and the good, and sends rain on the righteous and unrighteous." (Mt.5:43-45)

If we love the Lord God with all our heart, with our spirit, with our soul, with our mind, with our body, loving our neighbor is the natural result.

Chapter Twenty-Two

PRAYER FOR WORLD PEACE

God the Father Almighty, the creator of Heaven and Earth, the sea, and all that dwells in it-the forest and trees, mountains, rocks and the highest mountains on Earth-islands, valleys, sun, moon, stars that set and shine at its time, Rain and snow that fall at their season. The animals that run around in the forest, the birds that fly from one end of the Earth to another, the reptiles and tiny little ants that crawl on the ground. All these have their habitation in you O' Lord.

I pray with my whole heart, mind, body and spirit requesting that you reveal yourself to the people of all religions on Earth to give them great wisdom, understanding and knowledge to know that you are one God. I pray that you God of all the people on Earth, that Father, Son and Holy Spirit would reveal yourself to the idol worshipers that feel that they have to appease to the god of thunder, god of iron, worship the ocean and all the things you have created, instead of worshiping the creator who lives forevermore. Let the wars cease to include all the tribal wars, civil wars and nations against nations wars. Let them know that we are all brothers and sisters and that you are the one God and Father of all people on Earth.

Countries that are fighting each other because of a piece of land should know that you are the sole owner of every land on this Universe; we are all here temporary; everything is time under the Heavens. Let the presidents and the dictators of nations stop killing their own people because they do not want to leave their office, let them ask themselves where are the people before them. Pharaoh 3100 BC, Alexander the Great 496-168BC, Gaius Julius Caesar of the Roman Empire 100 BC, Napoleon Bonaparte Emperor of the French 1804-1815 and Dictator Adolf Hitler from Nazi Germany 1933-1945. Let them realize that when you take away your spirit from them, their money and position cannot return their spirit back to them. They are dead and gone forever.

Let love and unity prevail, beginning from the individual family, neighbors, community, city, states and may it spread to all the people in all the nations of Earth. Jesus Christ, the Prince of Peace, come quickly and bring us your perfect peace. Set up your kingdom on Earth; a new Earth where only righteousness rules forever. Hear our prayers O' Lord and bless this world of ours with peace. Bless all the children in the world; let them grow up with peace and love for each other; they are the next generation. Help us to stop the killing of children in all the war zones. Preserve the life of many children in the middle of the raging war. Great God of this Universe, let your peace that surpasses knowledge, position, money and fame rule the heart, mind, soul and body of all the people. Let them know that you are the ruler of all the souls of human being on Earth. Let the Holy Spirit of God continue to hover over the Earth with peace. In Jesus Christ's great and mighty Holy Name, I pray and everyone that reads this book says: Amen, Amen, Amen.

BIBILIOGRAPHY

Abdel Haleem, M.A. (2008). The qur'an oxford world's classics. Oxford University Press, Cary, NC USA.

Ali, M. M. (1991) Revised Edition. The holy qur'an with english translation and commentary. Ahamadiyya Anjuman Ishaat Islam Publishing Silver Spring, MD USA.

Berelin, Rabbi (2004). Torah, Talmud, and Jewish Law. The Destiny Foundation Press. New York, NY USA

Bank, R.D. (2002). The everything judaism book: A complete primer to the jewish faith from Holidays and rituals to traditions and culture. Adams Media Press. Avon, MA USA.

Barer, B. (2009). Judaism and the Baha'i Faith. Burl Barer Press. Rohnert Park CA, USA.

Berelwein, (Rabbi) (2004). Basic Book of Judaism: torah, Talmud, and jewish. The Destiny Foundation Press New York, NY, USA.

Carson, D. (2005) Second Edition. Crossing into medicine country: A journey in native american healing. Acade Publishing Company. New York, NY USA.

Doniger, W. (2010). The hindus: an alternative history. Penguin Books Chino Valley Arizona, USA.

Effendi, S. Advent of divine Justice. Bahai Publishing Trust Company, Wilmette, Chicago IL USA.

Esslemont, J.E. (2006). Introduction to baha'i faith. Bahai Publishing Trust Company Wilmett Chicago, IL USA.

Evans, A. L. (2006). Shinto Norito: A Book of Prayer by. Traffod Publishing IL, Chicago USA.

Flood, Gavin D. (1996). Additional Information: Divisions within Hinduism, the forehead mark, Hindu websites. Cambridge University Press, Shaftebury Cambridge, UK.

Flood, Gavin D. (1996). A General Introduction to Hinduism: Name of the religion, early history, sacred texts, beliefs, practices. Humanities Press Fremon, CA USA.

Hagen, S. (1998). Buddhism Plain and Simple. Broadway Books Division of Random House, Portland Oregon, USA.

Hollander, J. (1993). The Nineteenth Century, Vol. 2 Herman Melville to Stickney American Indian Poetry, Folk Songs and Spirituals. Library of America. New York, NY USA.

Jacobs, L. (1990). God Torah Israel Traditional Islam without Fundamentalism. Hebrew Union College Press. Cincinnati OH, USA.

Johnston, H. (2011). Witnesses to a world of crisis. historians and histories of the middle east in the seventh century. Oxford University Press. Cary, NC USA.

KolBrener, W. (2011). Open Minded Torah of irony, Fundamentalism and Love. Continuum International Publishing. Maiden Lane, NY USA.

Kulasrestha, M. (2007). The Golden Book of Jainism. Lotus Books Press Silver. Lake, WI USA.

Littleton, S. (2002). Shinto: origins, rituals, festivals, spirits, sacred places. Oxford University Press. Cary, NC USA.

Lopez, D.S. (2004). Buddhist Scriptures. Penguin Classics. One World Publications Oxford, London, UK.

Momen, M. (2007). A beginner's guide (one world). Penguin Classics Publishing. Chino Valley, Arizona USA.

Nausner, J. (2008). The Formative History of Judaism -Second Series, Studies in Judaism Questions and Answers. University Press of America. Emeryhlle, CA USA.

Nigosian, S. A. (1993). Zoroastrian Faith, Tradition and Modern Research. Mcgill Queens University Press. Montreal, Quebec, CANADA.

Mohammad, M. Ali (1991). Holy Qur'an English Trnslation & 7th Edition Commentary . Ahamadiyya Anjuman Ishaat Islam Publishing Silver. Spring, MD USA.

Patel, S.J. (2006). The Little Book of Hindu Deities: From the Goddess of Wealth to the Sacred Cow. Plume Publishers Div. of Penguine Group Publishing.

Pickthall, M. M. (2011). The meaning of the glorious koran. The New American Library, 12th Edition: Literary Licensing LLC Publishing. Houston, TX USA.

Shackle, C. &Mandair, A. (2005). Teaching of Sikh Gurus: Selections from the Sikh Scriptures. Routledge Publishing Taylor & Francis Group. Kentucky, USA.

Tobias, M. (2000). The world of jainism. Jain Publishing Company. Fremont, CA USA.

Yusuf Ali, A. (1997). An english interpretation of the holy qur'an english translation and full arabic text. Dar Ahya US – Sunnah al Nabawiya St. Anaheim CA, USA.

Yusuf Ali, A. (1997). The meanings of the illustrious qur'an with footnotes and an introduction of the qur'an. Dar Ahya US – Sunnah al Nabawiya Publishing. St. Anaheim CA, USA.

BIBLE REFERENCES

(1984), The Holy Bible, King James Version. Dugan Publishers, Inc. Winchester Hampshire, UK.

(1993), The Holy Bible, The New International Version Bible, Zondervan. Grand Rapids, MI USA.

Additional Information: Divisions within Hinduism, the forehead mark, Hindu websites. www.nolano.net/wwwgoof/hinduism.htm

FOOTNOTES

1. The relation between hunger, malnutrition, and other terms such as under-nutrition is not 'perfectly clear,' so we have attempted to spell them out briefly in "World Hunger Facts."

2. For example, the Oxford English Dictionary (1971 edition) has 'insufficient nutrition' as the only meaning for malnutrition.

3. For discussions of measuring hunger see Califero 2011, Headey 2011 and Masset, in press.

PERIODICALS AND OTHER MATERIALS

Black, RE; Morris, SS and Bryce, J. "Where and why are 10 million children dying every year?" *Lancet*. 2003 Jun 28; 361(9376):2226-34.

Black, Robert E; Allen; Lindsay H; Bhutta; Zulfiqar A; Caulfield; Laura E; De Onis, Mercedes ; Ezzati, Majid; Mathers, Colin & Juan Rivera, for the Maternal and Child Under-nutrition Study Group **Maternal and child under-nutrition: global and regional exposures and health consequences**. (Article access may require registration) *The Lancet* Vol. 371, Issue 9608, 19 January 2008, 243-260.

Bryce, Jennifer; Boschi-Pinto; Cynthia, Shibuya; Kenji & Robert E. Black, and the WHO Child Health

Cafiero, Carlo and Pietro Gennari. 2011. **The FAO indicator of the prevalence of undernourishment** FAO

Caulfield LE; De Onis, M; Blössner, M & Black, RE. **Under-nutrition as an underlying cause of child deaths associated with diarrhea, pneumonia, malaria, and measles**. *American Journal of Clinical Nutrition* 2004; 80: 193–98.

Chen, Shaohua & Ravallion, Martin, June 2004. "**How have the worlds poorest fared since the early 1980s?**" World Bank Policy Research Working Paper 3341 Washington: World Bank.

De Onis, Mercedes; Frongillo, Edward, A. & Blossner, Monika. 2000. "**Is malnutrition declining? An analysis of changes in levels of child malnutrition since 1980.**" *Bulletin of the World Health Organization* 2000, 1222–1233.

Food and Agriculture Organization, International Fund for Agricultural Development, World Food Program. 2002 "**Reducing Poverty and Hunger, the Critical Role of Financing for Food, Agriculture, and Rural Development.**"

Food and Agriculture Organization. 2006. **State of World Food Insecurity 2006** Report release October 14, 2009, 2008, 2006, 2005, 2002.

Epidemiology Reference Group. 2005. "**WHO estimates of the causes of death in children.**" *Lancet* ; 365: 1147–52.

Peter Svedberg, Professor at Oxford University Press 2000, **Poverty and Under-nutrition Theory, Measurement, and Policy.**

Loescher, Gil ; Betts, Alexander & Milner, James H., United Nations High Commissioner for Refugees 2008 Report. **The politics and practice of refugee protection into twenty first century**.

BIBLICAL INDEX

Gen. 16:20, 37:25-28, 12:13, 22:18, 39:1, 25:9, 22:16-18, 12:3, 22:18, 16:20, 37:25-28, 39:1, 25:9, 22:16-18, 21:17-19, 21:13, 1-3, 5, 16:1-5, 21:17-19,16:1-5, 21:13, 17:19

Dt. 18:15 /Job 32:8

Zch. 9:9

Dn. 9:25-26, 9:25-26

Is. 7:14, 2:3-4, 2:4; 9:6b-7, 11:3b-9, 12

Mc. 4:1-4

Mal. 4:6

Ps. 110:4

Mt. 5:9, 25: 31-45, 43-45

Mk. 12:28-31

Lk. 7:31-32, 1:35, 6:27-38, 23:46, 10:30-37, 22:16-18

Jn. 3:15, 4:24, 13:34-35

Heb. 10:10-14

Act. 7:59

Rm. 2:18-20, 1:21-22

HOLY QUR'AN INDEX

Holy Qur'an: 2:156-157

Holy Qur'an 2:183

Holy Qur'an: 2:201

Holy Qur'an: 2:255

Holy Qur'an: 21:47

Holy Qur'an: 33:56

Holy Qur'an 59:24

Holy Qur'an 66:6

Books previously
published by author
Grace Dola Balogun of
Grace Religious Books
Publishing &
Distributors, Inc.

Three Solutions for World Peace

**PRAYER THE SOURCE
OF STRENGTH FOR LIFE**
– **English Edition**

Prayer the Source of Strength for Life
is a powerful book that will energize our spirit
to pray more and more until the prayer is part
of your life and the gate of Heaven
is opened and your prayer is answered.
Your prayer will change your life.

LA ORACION FUENTE DE FORTALEZE PARA LA VIDA
Spanish Edition

Dios no's dio el poder de la oracion,quiere que lo usemos, debomos illamar,comunicarnos con el en todo lo queestemo spasando. El espera saber denosotros.

Three Solutions for World Peace

SPIRIT POWER VOL. I

Spirit Power, Volume I and II discuss the power of the Holy Spirit in the life of believers.

SPIRIT POWER VOL II

The power of the Spirit of God begins from the creation of the world up until today. That power will also continue until Christ returns to reign. Hallelujah!

THE CROSS AND THE CRUXIFIXION

Our Lord Jesus Christ died to bring forth love and compassion. Sin's impact on human life brings all other evil into our world, from one society to another, from one culture to another. But in Christ we are clothed with His holiness. We have the gift of eternal life. The gate of Heaven is open and we are eligible for our inheritance in Heaven. Hallelujah! Hosanna in the highest. Jesus Christ paid it all, unto Him all we owe. The Cross of Christ is the Cross of joy, peace and righteousness to all who believe in Him.

About the Author

Grace Dola Balogun graduated from Fordham University Graduate School of Religion and Religious Education in the year 2010 with an M.A. in Religion and Religious Education. She has been a prayer mentor and advisor for many Christians of all denominations for many years.

Visit her online at:

Gracereligiousbookspublishers.com

Prayerstrengthforlife.com

Spiritpower.infosalvationcompleted.com

Facebook

GSTwitter@prayersource

To Order This Book

To order additional copies of this book, please E-mail:
info@gracereligiousbookspublishers.com

This book may also be ordered from 30,000 wholesalers, retailers, and booksellers in the U. S., and in Canada and over 100 countries globally.

To contact Grace Dola Balogun for an interview or a speaking engagement, please E-mail:
info@gracereligiousbookspublishers.com

The Spirit and the bride say,
"Come!" And let the one who hears
say, "Come!" Let the one who is
thirsty come;
and let the one
who wishes take
the free gift of the
water of life.
(Revelation 22:17)

MARANATHA ! COME, LORD JESUS!

Three Solutions for World Peace

www.ingramcontent.com/pod-product-compliance
Lightning Source LLC
Chambersburg PA
CBHW051431290426
44109CB00016B/1507